Showcase 1

Plays from the Eugene O'Neill Foundation

Plays from the Eugene O'Neill Foundation

Edited by John Lahr

Who's Happy Now?

Oliver Hailey

The Indian Wants the Bronx

Israel Horovitz

Father Uxbridge Wants to Marry

Frank Gagliano

Muzeeka

John Guare

Grove Press, Inc. New York

Acknowledgments

Library of Congress Catalog Card Number: 76–100388

First Evergreen Black Cat Edition, 1970

Manufactured in the United States of America

The Eugene O'Neill Memorial Foundation is grateful to the Rockefeller Foundation whose generosity made a good idea a tangible reality.

Contents

Introduction by John Lahr 7

Who's Happy Now? by Oliver Hailey 11

The Indian Wants the Bronx by Israel Horovitz 87

Father Uxbridge Wants to Marry by Frank Gagliano 129

Muzeeka by John Guare 183

I

Introduction

America 1968–69 is a time of affluence. Despite war, stocks skyrocket; in spite of a Poor People's March on Washington, the majority is comforted by an ever-higher standard of living. It is a strange, paradoxical moment to be a playwright in the United States. In some ways, things have never looked better. A theater of protest has emerged—moving into the streets instead of away from them: guerrilla theater, black theater, even radical departures in style like the La Mama pieces under the direction of Tom O'Horgan, have found an audience and are thriving. Foundations have begun to support the theatrical enterprise. Young playwrights with luck and a surfeit of press clippings of predictable critical euphoria can look forward to a modest but helpful stipend. Now, at least, some playwrights can pay the rent as well as ply their craft. At the same time, the ruthless economics of entertainment make it difficult for the playwright to test his play, let alone mount it in a commercial production. The theater may be an appealing art form, but it is no longer a "popular" one. Television has assumed the voice of the masses, leaving the stage with both a loss and an opportunity. But experiment itself is not easy. The actors, the hall, the equipment have to be paid for, and unless they are of a high enough caliber, the enterprise dwindles to a bush-league adventure in which the playwright learns little for his trade. In a time of prosperity, the one thing which is needed for art, yet not conceded by the society, is the luxury of failure. How can the American theater develop its own tradition when financially every angle of production argues against even setting sail on such a treacherous journey? Playwrights are not only obsessed, they are masochistic.

The Eugene O'Neill Foundation at Waterford, Connecticut, is no panacea for a theatrical renaissance, but it has met the glaring needs of the playwright and the theater with action. It is different from most organizations of its ilk, demanding only raw talent and not success, wanting to expand the dialogue on theater instead of haranguing the world for one type of approach. The word "foundation" comes to the lips of theater people with a reverence which used to be reserved for God, or at least J. J. Shubert. The foundation is the American way of avoiding national subsidy of the arts. In an agnostic age, it has replaced the Church as patron, but still holds a kind of holy weight over those who must bow to its whims and committee decisions. The Government, at a time of unprecedented abundance, has not seen fit to support the theater—whose myopic social planning parallels the Government's ambivalent prosperity. While commercial theater is choking itself to death through economic pressures, the Government still forks out a humiliating 10 million dollars (England's national subsidy is above 40 million) and Big Business, whose tastes and profits have changed the intention of entertainment, contributes annually less than 1% of its allowable 5% tax-free deduction for the business of "culture."

Foundations have created a new breed of theatrical creator, for whom such terms as Ford, Rockefeller, Guggenheim have the salivary tinkle of Pavlov's bell. This is the inevitable result of a beast hungry to survive. It is neither sad nor promising. It is simply a fact of contemporary life, whose umbilical separation from industry is as great as its reliance on it. There is a new route for the actor, playwright, critic who wants to fulfill his artistic potential without burning his energy out as a garage attendant. It leads tortuously through the well-paneled offices of careful foundation executives who order prosciutto from the foundation dining room as avidly as they commission playwrights.

The path meanders through decision-making committees, yet hopefully will allow individual talent to develop unimpeded by the economic hazards no longer synonymous with the hardship thrill of "showbiz." The foundations may offer largesse, but their choices are as firmly fixed in "success" as the "hit-flop" Broadway criterion they attempt to avoid. It is a tricky situation. Grants go to talent that has somehow been proved. Talent becomes as much a question of fashion and the cash box as the public-approval barometer of *Variety*'s inane critical judgment.

The O'Neill Foundation is potentially different. It is loose, energetic, and active, dedicated not only to supporting theater, but to creating it. Inaugurated in 1965 by its director, George C. White, the O'Neill has become an umbrella for many theatrical enterprises—a National Theatre of the Deaf and the sponsor of a National Playwrights' Conference. The O'Neill's intentions differ from the recent governmental program to support a number of Broadway plays under the weather of bad or insensitive critical response. Its activity is centered not on nurturing the old audience, but on making a new one. In seeing a need and in formulating a direct program to fill it, the O'Neill in its short history has already made inroads into developing new talent and realistic theater concepts.

The Playwrights' Conference, held during three weeks of the summer, brings together professional directors, actors, critics, and up to twenty playwrights chosen from hundreds. Overlooking Long Island Sound, the O'Neill consists of a salty, whitewashed mansion, a barn, and a large stretch of field which rolls out like a green tongue toward the sea. It is the center of communication in the intense three weeks—sometimes fruitful, sometimes frustrating, but always pertinent. Playwrights do a lot of talking here, and a lot of rewriting. They can watch their work being rehearsed, hear it and see it in a staged reading or semi-full production. The O'Neill has a theater hewn from a reconverted barn, and an outdoor amphitheater. When the conference is in session, tents are pitched on the grounds so various productions can have their own private rehearsing space. The writer, usually holed up in a murky tenement, gets a chance to see the sun as well as his play, free room and board, and $50 a week. The actor, the victim of type casting and the decreasing number of New York plays, has a chance at two, sometimes three parts. And the critic (besides having the opportunity of hearing Edward Albee slap his wrist) finally manages to witness the complexity of the beast he so easily dismisses.

This anthology is an indication of the O'Neill's most conspicuous results. What cannot be tabulated is the experience, for an author, of working with special professionals, of adapting his intentions and his style. Five of the eighteen playwrights at the 1967 Conference received productions in New York or Los Angeles, but the work of the other thirteen is no less impressive, and the fruits for them will come later.

The O'Neill's growing importance is, in part, due to the immense vacuum it has filled for the new playwright. The talent might have emerged under its own strength, but not as quickly or under such propitious conditions. In 1968, O'Neill plays won two Vernon Rice Awards and two Obie Awards—a track record of imposing quality. The success itself poses problems: for the O'Neill will now have to struggle to keep its disenfranchised spirit, steer clear of the "hit" showcase with which journalists and theatrical entrepreneurs have begun to view it. As long as the O'Neill is prepared to take risks, it will remain above the swill of most foundations. In time, it may be necessary for the O'Neill to create its own repertory of actors as well as a touring company for its plays in order to sustain the atmosphere and the work accomplished in the Playwrights' Conference. This is all in keeping with its eclectic tastes and commitment to sustaining the magic of theater at a time when America, as well as its stage, must find new ways to cope, or die a slow, impoverished death.

—JOHN LAHR

Who's Happy Now?

Oliver Hailey

OLIVER HAILEY

". . . *Home sure do bring out the worst in people . . .*" (iii)

Who's Happy Now? is a conventional three-act comedy written with a perverse and hilarious consciousness that aspires to some aristocracy of instinct amid the banalities of a well-made play. In an American society which clings as avidly to the eternal verities of family, home, and sheltering of youth as it does to the proscenium arch, the Hallen ménage inverts a very middle class cliché that it pretends to inhabit. Mary and her boy, Sonny, come to meet the head of the family, Horse, on the only common ground—the local bar. It is in this sanguinary environment that Sonny (the narrator of the story) begins to understand the weird affection which blisters between mother, father, and Horse's outrageous mistress, Faye Precious, a twentieth-century appendage to some of Congreve's obtuse and lipsmacking ladies.

Hailey's success in *Who's Happy Now?* is not merely a mastery of conventional structure, but an informed tone which never loses its irony while at the same time conveying a genuine affection and warmth for the gargoyles of his imagination. Horse and Mary fight about their young son's eating habits—a parody of parental concern. Hailey has just the right turn of phrase for monstrous irony:

> MARY: All right, Sonny—it's time for your supper. (*She reaches into her purse, pulls out a half-pint of milk, a box of Post Toasties and a bowl.*)
>
> HORSE: Now ain't that a supper? No wonder he's such a runt.
>
> FAYE: Mrs. Hallen, you know you could bring him by the café just any night and I'd fix him a good hot supper. You, too.
>
> HORSE: The best!
>
> MARY (*as she serves* SONNY): This is perfectly fine—he has a hot lunch and a cold supper. Nobody needs a hot both.

Hailey's freshness with language matches the quirks of the characters' sentiments. Mary not only bristles at Horse's involvement with Faye Precious, she has a few words to say about her metier:

> I don't look like any WAITRESS. My mother would kill you saying I looked like a waitress. If there was one thing she didn't want Jane and me to be—well, it was two things—a waitress and a nurse. I can remember Jane lying down on the bed and crying, begging so hard for Mama to let her go to nursing school. But Mama stood over that bed and said bed is right—and bed is where you'll be if you become a nurse—or waitress. Those are the other two words for whore she said. Don't you ever call me a waitress again, Pop. I'm a married woman. And prouder of it than any waitress or nurse has to be of her calling.

Hailey manages to wedge pretensions of language with absurd distortions of self-regard. Horse recollects his family ties in lachrymose humor:

> HORSE (*hoisting the beer*): In memory of him! Betrayed by all but me! Married to the sorriest woman ever lived.

> RICHARD: Was my grandmother sorry?
> HORSE: A tramp of the first water . . .

Hailey succeeds in creating a world which operates on its own urgent, insane logic. Horse, the meat-cutter, a man with the sensitivity of a meat-grinder, has at the same time a crude appeal which makes him the ethos of his world. It is fitting and even logical that the birthday party of his forty-first year should have as its theme—meat. Wieners are strung like balloons across the ceiling; Mary bakes him a meat cake, and his boy decides to dedicate himself to his father's trade:

> I want your old set of tools. I want them for mine. I've decided to be a meat-cutter. Like you. I'm telling you tonight I'm becoming a meat-cutter—like my dad. Forever.

Horse's unabashed hatred for his son rarely varies; no situation can hide his impulse of disgust. Will Sonny write songs or be a meat-cutter? The questions of success and destiny to which every prep-school mentality has been diligently dedicated in the past century are turned topsy-turvy in Hailey's situation. Horse listens to one of Sonny's songs:

> RICHARD: It's no "White Christmas" Dad.
> FAYE: I sung it the best I could.
> MARY: He's just a boy—fourteen. A fourteen-year-old boy wrote that!
> HORSE: Shut up, Mary—he knows bad stuff when he hears it! He ain't the world's greatest meat-cutter, but he's not much of a songwriter either. Are you, boy?

Horse's dance, that final spirited canter across the stage which carries with it the energy, ignorance, and curious appeal of the man, has a focused control which recapitulates the irony and longing which infuse the play:

> HORSE: Can you dance, Mary?
> MARY: As well as you can, Horse.
> HORSE: I hope that's true!

He grabs her roughly by the waist, begins to swing her about the floor. They quickly pass FAYE *and* RICHARD. HORSE *shouts at* RICHARD.

How's this for dancing, boy?

RICHARD: It's fine, Papa. It's wonderful.

HORSE: You bet it is! Mary's as good a dancer as I am, by God.

The image, like the words, will not hold its solidity. Horse—that monumental ego—and Mary, the devoted wife, can never keep their love moving in the unison of the dance. The moment has its undeniable pathos. Sonny would like to freeze time and recall merely the sweetness. Hailey has sculptured a clever theatrical sleight-of-hand—finding insight in fun and language which comments on the characters as well as carries the story to its improbable conclusion. More than this, however, Hailey evokes an articulate despair—freeing parental memories from their clichés of youthful expression, to reveal something barren in the soul of every child who has yearned for love and known its quiet betrayal.

Who's Happy Now? was first performed at the Eugene O'Neill Memorial Theatre Foundation in Waterford, Connecticut, on August 4, 1967, during the Summer Playwrights' Conference. It was directed by Melvin Bernhardt. The lighting was by Pat Flynn, music by Michael Barr and lyrics by Dion McGregor. The stage manager was Rilla Bergman. The cast was as follows:

RICHARD	Charles Kimbrough
POP	John Coe
MARY	Tresa Hughes
HORSE	Tom Adkins
FAYE PRECIOUS	Peggy Pope

CHARACTERS

RICHARD

POP

MARY

HORSE

FAYE PRECIOUS

ACT ONE

SCENE: *The house lights go down. The curtains open on the set at half light. It is a barroom. The bar runs stage right. Downstage are two tables for two. Upstage right is a gaudy jukebox. Upstage center is the front door. Upstage left is a large window, also on the left wall, a door to the toilet. Downstage left is an upright piano. The bar's general décor makes it clear that America is in the midst of World War II. There is a large picture of FDR hanging above the bar, an American flag on one side of it, a Texas flag on the other side. A set of longhorns hangs above it. An UNCLE SAM WANTS YOU poster hangs near the door (someone has inserted the word EVEN between WANTS and YOU) and a WE SELL SAVINGS STAMPS sign by the cash register. "Welcome" in rope letters—hangs above the bar.* RICHARD, *a lean, good-looking fellow about thirty, enters from the rear of the audience, with a woman on his arm. He escorts her to a seat in the second row of the theater, then climbs onto the stage. He turns directly to the audience, smiles.*

RICHARD: My mother's here tonight. Stand up, Mama. (*He begins to clap for her as she stands briefly.*) I tried to get her to come to a rehearsal. She chose tonight. (*He makes a small shrug with his hands, then turns toward the set, glances at it for a moment.*) So the play will be different tonight. I'm the author and I can do what I wish with it. (*Beat.*) I'll be playing the boy—all three ages. Remember me at six, Mama? Act one. (*And then with a shout offstage.*) Okay. (*And he exits into the wings as the lights of the set come up fully, making it cozy, inviting.*)

The sound of wind begins, increases, howls. After a moment the front door opens and POP, *a wiry little man in his sixties, struggles in. With him comes a tumbleweed.* POP *hurls the tumbleweed outside again.* POP *is the bartender, wears an apron. The wind howls even louder while* POP *has the door open. He must struggle to shut it.*

POP: I'm blind. That dust blinded me! (*He goes behind the bar, fills a glass with what looks like a shot of whisky, splashes it in his eyes.*) I shouldn't of gone out. Only did to see if it was worth turning on the lights tonight. Only what do I get an eye full of? Her and that kid—headed right this way! Fighting their ways through that dust—they're being blowed from one side of that street to the other. (*He pushes the curtain aside, looks out the window.*) Just look at them out there! Oh hell, they're waving at me. What do they expect me to do—old man like me—run out there, swoop up two nondrinkers, bring them in here to safety? I will not! I'll close up first! That's what I should do on a night like this. Close up! (*He crosses to door, bolts it, pulls down the window shades. But then hesitates, raises the shades, unbolts the door.*) Except I take my calling seriously! This town is too small to close up its bar. Where would they go if I closed up? They'd stay home! I'll have you know more people kill each other in homes than ever do in bars! Homes bring out the worst in people. Especially in God-forsaken towns like this. (*Again he glances out the window.*) Sunray! Home of the played-out oil fields! (*He begins to dust the tables, which are covered with a layer of sand dust.*) Now ain't Sunray a name for this place!

Wonder who thought that one up? Man came through here once selling encyclopedias, he said it was ironic—a ironic name. And then explained to me what ironic is. Ironic is a town named Sunray—and it never sees one. (*At the window.*) And I'll give you another sample. Ironic is a woman with a six-year-old comes to a bar every night, and that woman don't drink!

The front door opens and MARY HALLEN, *a dark, subdued, but attractive woman in her thirties, enters with her son,* SONNY. RICHARD *plays the part of* SONNY, *with only suggestions that he is six years old. They, too, must fight the outside wind as they push the door shut.* MARY *carries an enormous duffel bag which she puts down by the front door. The boy looks up at his mother, crying.*

SONNY: I can't see. And my mouth is full of stuff, Mama.

MARY: Spit. Just spit, Sonny.

POP: Not on my floor, Mary.

MARY: Then here, Sonny. In this little can. (*She hands him a spittoon.*)

SONNY (*as* RICHARD, *moving downstage to his mother in the audience*): Have you ever been in a bar? In your life, Mama? Well . . . the whole play takes place in this bar. How's that for disguise? I told you I wouldn't tell it the way it happened. The play's full of disguises, Mama.

MARY: Did you see us waving?

POP: I did not!

SONNY: We both waved.

POP: I know you did, but I didn't see you!

MARY: Can we at least have a wet rag—to wipe our faces clean?

POP: I don't see why any teetotaler comes out on a night like this.

MARY: You close and we won't come out.

POP: I can't close just to keep you home. I got my business here.

MARY: And I got my business here!

SONNY *is making loud gagging sounds at the can.*

POP: Will you tell that kid not to vomit in there—just spit, please!

MARY: That's enough of that, Sonny. Come here—let me wipe your face. (*She reaches for him with the wet rag* POP *has given her.*) How's your throat?

SONNY: I still got stuff in my mouth. Look. (*He extends his tongue fully, then coughs.*)

MARY: Clear your throat and keep it clear. (*Wiping his mouth.*) I want your voice ready when I give the signal —remember?

SONNY: When will you give the signal?

MARY: We have to look for the right time.

POP: What are you up to, Mary Hallen?

MARY: A farewell surprise for Horse. Nothing to worry you.

POP (*with a glance at the duffel bag*): He gonna leave from here tonight?

MARY: We decided that was better than him coming back home and leaving from there.

POP: More natural, anyway. When was the last time Horse came home at night?

MARY: He comes home every night!

POP: When?

MARY: Finally! He always comes home! Don't try to make trouble, Pop.

POP: You're the troublemaker—in here every night!

SONNY: I want a drink, Mama.

POP: Glad to hear it! That's what this place is for—drinks! Step right up!

MARY (*suddenly enraged*): I swear to God, any man in this place ever give my boy another beer and I'll kill him! And that includes you and him and her!

POP: That's the chance you take when you bring a kid in a place like this!

MARY: Handing a child of six a bottle of beer and telling him it's orange soda pop. To this day Sonny won't go anywhere near orange soda pop! You've ruined orange soda pop for my boy.

SONNY: I want a drink, Mama.

MARY: Sonny, don't say drink. In here. Say water.

SONNY: I was hoping for soda pop. (*In a whisper.*) Any color but orange.

POP (*leaning over the counter at Sonny*): We don't sell soda pop—no color! This ain't a soda pop place! You don't make money off soda pop!

MARY: You keep Coca-Colas and you give him one right now. And you give me one, too! I know you keep them. I've seen a certain somebody drinking them!

POP: Where's your dime?

MARY *opens her purse, proudly displays a bill.*

MARY: Here's my dime! Where's your change for a twenty-dollar bill?

POP: He give you that money? Horse give you that to blow? Because he's leaving?

MARY: None of your business. That's business between a man and his wife! Just be fast with my change.

POP: I never knew you to get any money. Horse says butchers don't make enough money to give their wives any.

MARY: Just get our Cokes, please. That's your business! And make sure they're cold. (MARY *takes a toothbrush out of her purse.* SONNY *picks up the toothbrush.* MARY *slaps his hand.*) Leave your Daddy's toothbrush alone! (*Examining the toothbrush.*) I should've bought him a new one out of my twenty.

As POP *goes for the Cokes,* MARY *begins to unwind her hair, which is extremely long, and which she usually wears in a large bun at the back.*

POP (*noticing as she unwinds it*): You should let your hair down more often, Mary.

MARY: It came undone in the wind.

POP: You look good that way.

MARY (*removing a brush from her purse, combing her hair somewhat vainly*) : I know I do.

POP : You used to wear it that way all the time. I know why you stopped.

MARY : I chose to stop.

POP : Horse caught that salesman fooling with it, didn't he?

MARY (*suddenly pulling her hair to her, as if it had been bothered*) : Sonny—did you understand any of that?

SONNY : No, Mama.

MARY : Go play with the jukebox. (SONNY *moves to the jukebox*). I chose to stop. I came to realize some men have no control when it comes to long, beautiful hair. (*She combs proudly.*)

POP : What was that salesman doing—when Horse caught him?

MARY : That salesman had no control.

POP : What was he doing?

MARY : Pop, some things are so personal between a man and his wife a bartender has no right knowing them—but I'll tell you, anyway. Because I'm sick of your innuendoes!

POP : My what? Is that Mexican? A Mexican word? Watch out! I know Mexican!

MARY : I let Horse catch that salesman! Deliberately let Horse catch him running fingers through my hair.

POP : That all he was doing? Running his fingers through it?

MARY : Every week. It was like an obsession. Every week. He'd come in the store to sell Horse an order of meat, and he'd sneak those fingers into my hair. When Horse wasn't looking, of course. I kept asking him to stop—to use control—Horse would kill him if he caught him. Well, he said he was running his hand through hair up and down the state, and most of the wives seemed to appreciate it.

POP : Did you appreciate it?

MARY : I said I appreciated it, but I didn't like it. And my husband wouldn't like it either. He said not to be so sure about that, oftentimes it was surprising how the husbands seemed to appreciate it too.

POP: Not Horse.

MARY: I said Horse wouldn't, he said I might be surprised. I said why don't you do it in front of him and see, he said he just might, I said do! About that time Horse came out of the icebox, I turned my back to the salesman, my hair just flowing down before him, and he being a man of no little temptation, he began to run those fingers up and down my hair, up and down my hair. (*She makes a running gesture with her finger.*) Then we both turned to Horse, all the time those fingers going in and out of my hair.

POP: Yeh?

MARY: Well, a big smile crossed Horse's face. And then he said to the salesman, let me take your hand. And the man turned to me, and he said, see, I told you you might be surprised. And so he let go of me and gave the hand to Horse, and Horse grabbed hold of it, slammed it on the block and chopped off two fingers!

POP: Horse is a fine man with a cleaver. I just wish I could've seen it.

MARY: I remember one finger landed in Mrs. Worsham's grocery basket. She about died. But Horse was within his rights. The insurance company said so. They didn't have to pay that salesman a penny. Not even for the one they couldn't sew back on.

POP (*turning to* SONNY): You got yourself a papa, boy!

SONNY: When's Papa coming?

MARY (*quietly*): Shut up.

POP: I hear Faye Precious is having to close up the café this week. Mrs. Moot is on vacation.

MARY: Where'd she go?

POP: She said she was going home to bed. That's what Mr. Moot wanted. "I just want you to come home and get in bed with me, Mrs. Moot." When people can get that happy in bed, it's sad they have to get out of it—ain't it?

MARY: I've thought that.
POP: *You* have?
MARY: Yes. I have.
POP: I guess anybody who's ever been in bed's thought it. (MARY *crosses moodily to the window, looks out.*) You know what Mrs. Moot said last week? You and Faye Precious look alike. A little. She said.
MARY: I don't look like any WAITRESS! My mother would kill you saying I looked like a waitress. If there was one thing she didn't want Jane and me to be—well, it was two things—a waitress and a nurse. I can remember Jane lying down on the bed and crying, begging so hard for Mama to let her go to nursing school. But Mama stood over that bed and said bed is right—and bed is where you'll be if you become a nurse—or a waitress. Those are the other two words for whore, she said. Don't you ever call me a waitress again, Pop. I'm a married woman. And prouder of it than any waitress or nurse has to be of her calling.

Suddenly the front door is pushed open and HORSE *enters, followed by* FAYE PRECIOUS. *She is slightly younger than* MARY *and* HORSE, *vividly made up.* HORSE *is a large, boisterous man in his mid-thirties.*

SONNY: Hi, Papa.
HORSE: Hi, hamburger!
SONNY: Don't call me hamburger!
HORSE (*to* MARY): No weather too bad to bring him out?
MARY: He has the right to spend the evening with his father . . . doesn't he?
FAYE: Of course he does. (*She crosses to* SONNY, *pats his chin.*) Every little boy does.
SONNY: Mama, she touched me.
MARY: Don't touch him, Faye Precious.
FAYE: Sorry, Mrs. Hallen.
MARY: All right, Sonny—it's time for your supper. (*She*

reaches into her purse, pulls out a half pint of milk, box of Post Toasties and a bowl.)

HORSE: Now ain't that a supper? No wonder he's such a runt.

FAYE: Mrs. Hallen, you know you could bring him by the café just any night and I'd fix him a good hot supper. You, too.

HORSE: The best!

MARY (*as she serves* SONNY): This is perfectly fine—he has a hot lunch and a cold supper. Nobody needs a hot both.

HORSE: That woman never would fix me a hot supper.

MARY: There's always somebody to do it, isn't there?

FAYE (*anxious to change the topic, taking off her hat and beginning to examine it*): Oh—my feather! I shouldn't of worn it! But I do like to dress up a little in the evenings. Poor feather.

HORSE: I'll buy you another feather, Faye Precious. (*He yanks the feather from her hat, throws it away.*)

FAYE: Don't talk like that, Horse. (*Turning quickly to* MARY.) He's never bought me a thing, Mrs. Hallen. Don't let him get your goat. I wouldn't let him buy me anything. You know I wouldn't. Waitresses make enough.

HORSE: Two beers, Pop!

FAYE: Oh, can't I have a Coke, Horse? Please!

HORSE: No. Beer!

POP: Horse—you're in a mean mood tonight.

HORSE: I'm in a mean mood every night—once I get a sight of her and him. (*He stares at* MARY *and* SONNY.) Two beers—and hurry!

POP: But it don't mean you gotta take it out on Faye Precious —force her to drink beer!

FAYE: No—it don't, Horse!

HORSE: I ain't gonna be the only person in this bar drinking! Two is gonna drink! Me and Faye Precious!

FAYE: How come it's gotta be us two all the time?

HORSE: Get those beers up here, Pop!

POP: No! I won't serve beer to them what don't want it!

MARY: Yeh? What about my boy? You served him, didn't you? And he didn't want it! If you'll serve children don't want it, you should serve grown women don't want it either.

HORSE: Yeh—you sure should! Damn good point, Mary! We got you there, Pop!

POP (*serving two beers*): Yeh—you got me! (FAYE PRECIOUS *gives* MARY *a hurt glance as she accepts her beer.*) I'm sorry, Faye Precious. I'd put some flavoring in it if it was anything else. But there's nothing you can do to beer.

FAYE: Oh, I know. Why God came up with beer—after he'd invented chocolate and Coca-Cola, I don't know!

HORSE: Just take big swallows, Faye Precious. And don't whine.

FAYE (*groaning in the face of her beer*): That's not whining —that's gagging. (*But finally taking as big a swallow as she can manage.*) Oh, my—oh, my, my! (*She turns to* MARY.) You're a lucky woman, Mrs. Hallen.

MARY (*nodding*): I do enjoy a Coke in the evening.

HORSE: Already spending your money, I see.

POP: I asked her how come you dropped a fortune on her, but she wouldn't tell me. Or did you know she's got a twenty-dollar bill?

HORSE: I know it and I don't like it, but it's the law, Pop! While I'm gone, they'll be sending her money right out of my pay check. Allotments they call it. So much of my money every month. (*He stares at* MARY.) Hers to spend as she pleases! And just look at her—already blowing it to Coke!

POP: She's already got a allotment check?

HORSE: No—but I got to leave her something, don't I? I thought I'd give it to her tonight and see how she handled herself. (*With a roar.*) Well, you're handling yourself pretty poorly, Mary!

MARY: Would you like to play the jukebox, Sonny?

HORSE: That lousy noisemaker—no! I won't have that thing

going! (*And then to* FAYE PRECIOUS, *who is struggling with her beer.*) And stop spitting beer, Faye Precious!

SONNY: I love that box, Mama.

MARY: I know you do, honey. Here. (*She hands him a nickel and he runs to the jukebox.*)

HORSE: So help me, you put that nickel in there, hamburger, and I'll dance with Faye Precious!

FAYE: Oh, please, no—no! I'm feeling a little woozy, Horse.

POP: No dancing in here, Horse! Law doesn't allow it.

HORSE: You turn it into a music dance hall with that no-good machine and I'll dance! I'm warning you, Mary, I'll dance with Faye Precious and I'll hold her tight! I will!

FAYE: Oh, my goodness.

MARY: You think I care?

HORSE: I know you care! You always have and you always will! Because you're my wife! Face that, Mary. Face it! (MARY *stares at him for another moment. Watching her hesitation, a smug smile crosses his face. Seeing this, she turns abruptly to* SONNY, *nods her permission to put the nickel in the jukebox.* SONNY *does. "Your Secret Is Safe With Me," a Western jump tune, blares forth.* HORSE *quickly grabs* FAYE PRECIOUS *by the arm, yanks her from her chair.*) Okay, Faye Precious—you asked for it!

FAYE: I didn't do a thing, Horse! (*As* HORSE *swings her past* MARY.) Oh, Mrs. Hallen, you've really got it in for me, haven't you?

HORSE *dances* FAYE PRECIOUS *wildly about the room. He is as inept as he is vigorous.*

POP (*following them—almost as if the three of them were dancing*): Stop it, Horse! You can't do that! It's against the law! Dancing's against the law in here!

MARY: Come on, Pop—who'd call what he's doing dancing?

HORSE: I'm dancing!

MARY: You're jumping and hugging!

POP: Okay, Horse—you asked for it! (POP *moves to the jukebox, unplugs it. The music stops abruptly.*)

FAYE: Thank goodness! (*But then she grabs her stomach.*) Oh, I'm sick! I'm sick!

HORSE: Is that beer you're spittin'?

FAYE (*running toward the toilet door*): Among other things!

HORSE: Faye Precious, will you never learn!

FAYE: Will *you* never learn! Did it ever occur to you maybe you expect too much from women! (*She bangs shut the rest-room door.* HORSE *begins to pound on it. She throws it open, roars.*) Well, you do!

She slams the door again. HORSE *pounds again. A beat later this sound is duplicated by* MARY *pounding on the jukebox for her nickel to return. But it does not, so she crosses to* POP.

MARY: Give me back my nickel, Pop.

POP: What nickel?

MARY (*she points to the jukebox*): The song wasn't over when you unplugged it.

POP: I had to. The law.

MARY: I didn't break it. And I didn't get my nickel's worth.

POP (*grudgingly giving her the nickel*): You're a hard woman with money, Mary Hallen.

MARY: I'm a good woman with money. What do you think, Horse?

HORSE: I like what I just seen, yeh.

MARY: Sit at our table a little. While she's in there.

HORSE: Why?

MARY: I'll buy you a beer.

HORSE: Out of your money?

MARY: Yes.

HORSE: That's got to last you a month—twenty dollars.

MARY: I know it.

HORSE: Hell, yes, I'd like a beer out of your money, Mary. (*He sits with them.*)

SONNY: Hi, Papa.

HORSE: Hi, hamb—— boy.

SONNY *beams.*

MARY: Pop—two beers and another Coke!

HORSE: Two beers?

MARY: I'll try. As my good-bye present to you.

HORSE: Well, damn you, Mary! (*He slaps her on the back, gets a handful of her long, flowing hair.*) Aren't you wearing your hair a little different?

MARY: Tonight being your last for awhile, I thought maybe you'd enjoy it this way. (*She fluffs the hair toward him.*)

HORSE: Maybe I will and maybe I won't. Don't push me, Mary.

There is a pause as SONNY *makes a whistling sound by blowing into his Coke bottle.*

MARY: I don't push. Sonny, why don't you take off your papa's shoes . . . Make him more comfortable. (*She points toward Horse's feet.* SONNY *misunderstands.*)

SONNY (*a loud stage whisper*): Is that the signal? Ready for me to do it?

MARY: Not yet. Just take off his shoes now.

SONNY *straddles Horse's leg, removes a boot—then the other boot.* HORSE *cannot resist giving* SONNY *a kick with the removal of the second boot. But* SONNY *happily cradles Horse's feet in his lap.* POP *brings the beers and Coke.* MARY *and* HORSE *lift their beers.*

HORSE (*offering his beer as a toast to her*): Damn you, Mary!

MARY: Thank you, Horse.

HORSE *and* MARY *sip their beers,* SONNY *drinks his Coke. Slowly* HORSE *reaches over as if to kiss* MARY. *But before they can kiss,* RICHARD *rises, stops them.*

RICHARD: No—I don't want the kiss in the play. Remember that time, Mama? It was at the Walkers' picnic. You did try to drink beer. You were ashamed afterwards. But I was proud of you. And it was the only time I ever saw you kiss him. The kiss isn't in the play tonight. We've tried it, but it doesn't look real. But it was real—that time you kissed him. Admit it. (*He sits again, assumes his role as* SONNY.)

HORSE: I'll say one thing for you, Mary—you're not spitting your beer.

SONNY: She's drinking beer! You're drinking beer, Mama—did you know that?

MARY: Yes—I know.

SONNY: Does it taste good, Mama?

MARY (*again with her eye on* HORSE): It's tasty.

HORSE (*slaps* MARY *on the back again*): You're all right, Mary! I just may buy *you* one.

She gives a smile that betrays that one is quite enough.

SONNY. I'll be glad when I can drink beer.

MARY: Don't say that! Horse, don't let him say that.

HORSE: Don't ruin the party, you little brat!

SONNY: I did taste it once—didn't I, Mama? Once.

MARY *puts her beer down, stares hard at* HORSE. HORSE *looks at her, then turns to* SONNY.

HORSE: You're really out to ruin the party, aren't you, hamburger? Get lost, you little bastard! Leave my wife and me alone.

MARY: Don't talk to him like that, Horse!

HORSE: He's ruining our party!

MARY: It's not a party.

HORSE: It could be. Sometimes. If we could ever shake him.

MARY: We don't have parties.

HORSE: I have parties! (*He suddenly runs his fingers through Mary's hair—roughly. She rises abruptly, turns away, ties her hair up again.* HORSE *shouts.*) Faye Precious, get back in here!

SONNY *turns around in his chair, away from* HORSE.

MARY: Don't cry, Sonny.

HORSE: You cry and I'll whack you, hamburger!

MARY: You won't.

SONNY: He will.

MARY: Why can't you ever treat him nice?

HORSE: Because I don't like him. I just don't like him. I've never liked the kid. That's why.

SONNY (*as* RICHARD): I know it sounds too mean, Mama. I know *he* had a *special* way of saying it. (*And then to audience.*) It was almost like a carnival barker does—when he's got the best attraction on the midway. "I don't like him! I just don't like him! I've never liked the kid! Right this way!" The way we're doing it, I feel like an orphan. (*He pats the actor playing* HORSE *consolingly on the arm, then resumes his position.*)

HORSE (*attempting to duplicate the way* RICHARD *has delivered the line*): I don't like him. I just don't like him. I've never liked the kid.

RICHARD *nods approvingly to his mother in the audience.*

MARY: Okay, Sonny. Now. Now.

SONNY: What?

MARY: You know. It.

SONNY: Oh—the song! Now? Hot dog!

MARY: Don't say it—just do it.

HORSE: I don't like songs!

MARY: You're not going to believe this, Horse—he did it all by himself. Practically.

HORSE: Did what?

MARY: The little tune, the rhymes—he rhymed it—he did it all. Go on, Sonny—sing it.

HORSE: I don't like songs, Mary.

MARY: Shut up and listen, Horse! It's your good-bye song. Okay, Sonny—sing it! (MARY *sits at the piano, begins to play.*)

SONNY:

My name is Sonny
And I'm from Sunray
Born on a Sunday afternoon
Sunray's a sun town

Sunup and sundown
When there's a Sunray Texas moon.

My name is Sonny
I'm Mama's sunbeam
I'm Mama's sunbeam ev'ry day
And very sun-glad
To have a sun-dad
In Sunray, Texas, U.S.A.

At the song's conclusion applause is heard from FAYE PRECIOUS—*standing at the toilet door.*

FAYE: That's wonderful! Just wonderful, Sonny!
MARY: And he did the rhymes by himself practically.
HORSE: What are rhymes?
MARY: Sun-glad and sun-dad—that's what rhymes are. Glad and dad happen to rhyme. And Sonny thought them up.
HORSE (*to* SONNY): You did that?
SONNY: Yes, sir.

There is a silent moment as the two stare at one another —evaluate one another. Then HORSE *turns away in disgust.*

FAYE: It's just wonderful! Let me sing it—can I?

My name is Sonny
And I'm from Sunray—

SONNY: No, you can't sing it! Stop her, Mama!
FAYE: Why can't I?
SONNY: Your name's not Sonny, that's why.
MARY: Sonny—you should be proud someone wants to sing your song.
SONNY: Do we like her, Mama?
MARY: You should be glad anyone wants to sing your song. Sing it, Faye Precious.
FAYE: Thank you, Mrs. Hallen.

My name is Sonny
And I'm—

SONNY: Your name's still not Sonny!

HORSE *gives the boy an angry glare—points a finger for the boy to behave himself.*

FAYE (*She glares at* SONNY *for a moment, then begins again —*MARY *at the piano*):
His name is Sonny
And he's from Sunray
Born on a Sunday afternoon
Sunray's a sun town
Sunup and sundown
When there's a Sunray Texas moon.

Come on, join me, Sonny. We'll make a little harmony.

He hesitates, glances at his mother. MARY *hits a couple of notes of harmony to encourage him.*

FAYE & SONNY:
My name is Sonny
I'm Mama's sunbeam
I'm Mama's sunbeam ev'ry day
And very sun-glad
To have a sun-dad
In Sunray, Texas, U.S.A.

FAYE (*she hugs* SONNY): You're a genius, Sonny! You are!
SONNY (*wrapped in Faye Precious' embrace—struggling to speak to his mother*): Mama—she's touching—
MARY: It's all right, Sonny. She appreciates your talent.
HORSE (*watching* FAYE *hug* SONNY, *moving to them, shouting proudly*): Beer and steer!
FAYE: What?
MARY: Horse just made a rhyme. Sit down, Horse.
SONNY: It's a good rhyme, Papa.
HORSE: I didn't ask you! You shut up!
MARY: Anybody can rhyme words. The trick is to put them into songs.
HORSE: Well, it's a dumb trick and it ain't my trick maybe.

MARY: Certainly isn't.

HORSE: Thank God! My trick happens to be breaking down a beef! (*To* SONNY.) Can you do that? Can anybody here do that? Speak up! Anybody?

FAYE: My, no, Horse—I can't even bear to watch you do it.

HORSE: Why can't you watch? Something wrong with breaking down a beef? You think something's wrong with it?

FAYE: 'Course I don't.

HORSE: Juries do. They won't put a butcher on a jury. They think he's too cruel to be on a jury. Did you know that? (*This is* not *spoken to* POP.)

POP: Yeh—I knew it.

HORSE: Oh, boy, it hurt me when I found that out!

FAYE: I didn't mean nothing like that, Horse. It just makes me a little woozy to watch you do it.

HORSE: Lots of things make you woozy, Faye Precious. (FAYE PRECIOUS *looks at him for a moment, then suddenly turns away, begins to sob.*) You crying, Faye Precious?

FAYE: I was thinking of my late husband, and what used to make him woozy. So woozy he'd lose his stomach. Every time. (*She sobs loudly.*)

POP: What?

FAYE: He said he'd die if I ever told. Of course . . . now he's dead. (*Another sob.*)

HORSE: Tell it! What was it?

FAYE (*a pause*): Love. Love is what made him woozy.

MARY: Love?

FAYE: Making it.

MARY: Sonny, go to the bathroom.

SONNY: I don't need to!

HORSE: Get in there and *try!*

SONNY *obeys.*

FAYE: I was careful as I could be about the way I said it, Mrs. Hallen.

HORSE: She hasn't even said it. You get it, Pop?

POP (*snickering*): I think I do.

HORSE: I think I do too. You telling us, Faye Precious, every time this old fellow took you to bed, then he'd have to get right back up, go to the—

FAYE: That's enough, Horse!

POP: Every time, Faye Precious?

FAYE (*crying*): From the wedding night on. I was so innocent, for the first few weeks I just thought that was part of it. And I felt so sorry for men. But then he came to me, poor worn-out thing, and he said, "Faye Precious, I just can't keep this up."

HORSE: Should of said he just couldn't keep it down!

FAYE: Horse—please!

POP: So what happened?

MARY: No details, Faye Precious.

FAYE: It's okay, Mrs. Hallen. It's not a bad answer. We just vowed to give it up, my husband and me.

MARY: Give it up?

HORSE: Hell!

FAYE (*crying*): He told me he was sorry as he could be, he'd looked forward to it all his life . . . but now it was here . . . well, it just wasn't what he'd hoped it'd be. And we'd have to stop, or he might die from it. And you could see he was already beginning to waste away.

POP: So you gave it up?

HORSE: Nobody can give it up.

MARY: Could you, Faye Precious?

FAYE: Well, we were doing real fine. For three weeks. Only then—three weeks to the day after we made the vow—my husband fell off his rigging and was killed.

HORSE: That's the only way you can give it up.

FAYE: I've just had an awful life, haven't I?

HORSE: It's an awful story, Faye Precious. Damn, I'm depressed! Give me a beer, Pop.

FAYE (*still crying*): I didn't mean to depress you, Horse. But . . . well . . . life happens to be a little depressing.

HORSE: You think I don't already know that? I'm going in the U.S. Army this very night, ain't I? To kill Japs and

Germans. All because my wife had three miscarriages and I end up with only one kid and am eligible for the draft! I know life is depressing! Why do you think I bring you here every night?

FAYE: I'm sorry, Horse. Maybe if I sang for you?

HORSE: I hate songs!

FAYE: It's the best thing I do.

HORSE: It is not!

FAYE: See—you're cheering up already. (*She laughs, takes his hand.*)

POP: You could've been a singer, Faye Precious, 'stead of a waitress if you'd wanted. (*He has aimed this remark at* MARY.)

FAYE: I know it. Several of my regular customers will not eat until I have sung.

HORSE: Singing is not the thing Faye Precious does best!

FAYE: I wish you would please not talk that way in front of Mrs. Hallen, Horse.

MARY: I'm used to it, Faye Precious.

FAYE: I don't see how you *got* used to it, Mrs. Hallen. It still embarrasses me to death—everything Horse says about him and me in front of you. Why, every night I come through that door and see you and the boy sitting here again, I just want to die!

MARY: You'd feel better if the boy and I stayed home?

FAYE: Oh—a lot better! Why don't you try that some night, Mrs. Hallen? Huh?

HORSE: You think I haven't told her to stay home? You tell her—see where it gets you!

MARY: We've stayed home, Faye Precious.

FAYE: When? I can't remember you missing a night.

MARY: At first. We tried staying home. But it's no life for the boy—at home. He falls asleep before Horse gets there. Now me—I don't. I always wait up.

FAYE: You wait up for Horse every night? I don't think I knew that.

MARY: I'm married to him. I'm the last one to see him—every night.

FAYE: Well, that's nice.

MARY: But I bring the boy here so he can know his father too.

SONNY (*entering from the toilet*): Yeh—and this place has the jukebox. (*He runs to the jukebox, begins to punch the selection buttons.*)

POP: You bet it does! This is a first-class place!

MARY: This is the only place the boy gets a chance to know Horse. But I know Horse at home—every night.

HORSE: Shut your mouth, Mary.

FAYE: Oh, my goodness, Horse, can't you behave when she and me are getting to where we can talk a little? After all, you're going tonight. That'll just leave her and me and the boy here. If you expect us all to be waiting for you when you get back, you might want us to get on a little better footing before you go.

HORSE: I won't be coming back! I'll get killed. You watch. If a German doesn't get me, a Jap will.

MARY: You won't get killed.

HORSE: How do you know?

MARY: I only know what you've always said.

HORSE: What have I said?

MARY: About your father.

HORSE: Why, Mary, that's right! I'm thirty-three! The war won't last seven years, will it? Anybody here think the war'll last seven years?

POP: The last one only lasted four.

HORSE: Sure it did—four's enough! Mary, you've cheered me up!

FAYE: How did she do it?

HORSE: My dad died when he was forty!

FAYE: Yeh?

HORSE: Well . . . don't you see . . . I'll die when I'm forty!

FAYE: How come?

HORSE: How come? Because I loved him! I loved the hell out

of him! Damn, I loved him! And it's not easy for me to say something like that, is it, Mary?

MARY: No.

HORSE: Oh, Mary—I'm thinking about him, damn it. I'm thinking about him again! (*He begins to cry—heaving.*) Help me stop it! Help me!

His head falls on the table with the sobs. MARY *rises from her table, crosses to him.*

MARY: Think about him a little. It's okay. It'll go away in a minute.

HORSE *reaches for Mary's hand—squeezes it tightly.*

FAYE (*softly—to* MARY): What kind of a man was his father—just wonderful?

MARY *nods affirmatively.*

HORSE (*from deep within his sobs—beating a fist on the table*): Wonderful! Wonderful! (*Another moment of sobs, and then he lifts his head, wipes an eye.*) I'm going to tell her what he was, Mary—okay? Just tell her what he was.

MARY: He was a lawyer, Faye Precious.

HORSE: That's all I'm telling you. A lawyer. I'm a meat-cutter and he was a lawyer. That's enough to say, ain't it, Faye Precious?

FAYE: Oh—it's fascinating.

Horse's head falls on the table again as he struggles to gain control. SONNY *rises and moves to him.*

SONNY: Don't cry, Papa—please.

HORSE (*his head still lowered*): You get away! Get away! (*Again he is crying.*) Mary, keep him away from me!

MARY *signals to* SONNY *to move away, but* SONNY *stands firm.*

SONNY (*as if by rote*): When you break down the beef, you break it into halves and then into the front quarter and the hindquarter. In the front quarter you get the shoulder roasts and the club steaks. And in the hindquarter you get the T-bones, and then the sirloins, and then the round steaks and the rump roast. Right, Papa?

HORSE (*slowly looking up*): How'd you learn that? (SONNY *remains silent.*) How'd he learn it, Mary? How?

MARY: He's a bright boy, I've been telling you. He sees the charts on your back wall and . . .

HORSE: Who told him to learn them? I know grown meat-cutters never learned them. Mary, you taught them to him—didn't you?

MARY: Give the boy credit, Horse.

HORSE: Damn you, Mary. Damn my boy, too! There are full-grown meat-cutters don't know that stuff! (*He suddenly pulls* SONNY *to him.*) I hope to hell I don't get killed by a Jap or a German. I hope I get to come back and see you full grown, boy.

MARY: You will. Remember your father.

HORSE (*another sob*): Oh, I do remember him, Mary. I always will. Just like I hope my boy will always remember me.

SONNY: Oh—I won't forget *you*.

HORSE *holds* SONNY *tightly with one arm,* MARY *with the other.* FAYE PRECIOUS *crosses hesitantly to join them, touches Horse's hand gently in order to be included in the picture.* HORSE *reaches out, takes her hand, squeezes it. She sits beside them, continuing to hold his hand. They all pause in position for a moment, as if it were a picture. But then the honking of a bus is heard—three times.* HORSE *rises in silence, crosses to the bar without glancing at any of them, picks up his duffel bag and exits bravely.* FAYE PRECIOUS, MARY, SONNY *and* POP *all stare forward in silence, their sense of loneliness increasing as*

HORSE *exits.* RICHARD *moves to the forestage as a scrim is slowly lowered, those remaining on the stage illuminated behind it. A spotlight hits* RICHARD.

RICHARD: Remember that night? (*He stares into the second row.*) Those are lovely nights, aren't they—when men go off to war? But a lot of those men live—and they come home again. Don't they, Mama?

The spotlight goes out. The stage goes to dark. RICHARD *exits. The house lights come up.*

ACT TWO

SCENE: *It is now 1951, the bar's décor has been changed somewhat. The large photograph of FDR has been replaced by one of Harry Truman. The UNCLE SAM WANTS YOU and WE SELL SAVINGS STAMPS signs have been removed. "Welcome" has faded considerably, indicating that the word has hung for several years.*

These permanent décor touches, however, are secondary to the bar's current disarray, which consists of assorted party supplies scattered about the counter and on the tables—ribbons, meat hooks, a box of wieners, a stack of white aprons and butcher hats, a bag of sawdust, a rope, a rake.

POP *stands at the counter surveying the room with disgust.* RICHARD *crosses to a box, begins to remove meat hooks, tie them to the rope.*

POP: What are you doing with *them?*

RICHARD: Going to hang wieners from the ceiling. Two rows maybe—crisscross. You scatter the sawdust. I sneaked out his rake. (*He points toward the rake in the corner.*)

POP (*moving to scatter sawdust*): You think this'll put Horse in a party mood? Work all day, come over here and find his bar's been turned into another meat market?

RICHARD: I wish we had meat blocks—instead of tables. Fancy cafés do that sometimes.

POP: Meat blocks? You're lying to me, boy.
RICHARD: I read it in a book!
POP: No wonder he hates you—you sure are a smart ass.
RICHARD: I can't help reading.
POP: 'Course you can! Why can't you?
RICHARD: Once you learn how, it's a habit. If you'd learned how, you'd know what I mean.
POP: I can read! (*He points to the large rope word.*) Welcome!
RICHARD: I mean sentences.
POP: Oh. (*A pause as he stares at Richard.*) You want you and Horse to be pals, you know what I'd do? Give up reading!
RICHARD: I couldn't give up reading.
POP: Try: You ain't tried! Do it like Alcoholics Anonymous —they just promise not to drink today, that's all. You promise not to read today. And from day to day. You can make it—I know you can!
RICHARD: It doesn't bother you you can't read?
POP: I can read words and I don't miss sentences.
RICHARD: That's the way Horse is, he knows lots of words.
POP: Sure, and you hang onto the ones you already got. Most of 'em. Might dump a few of the fancy ones. Like bane of our existence.
RICHARD: You remember that?
POP: You hurt Horse awful calling him that. When he found out what bane meant, he was hurt.
RICHARD: I went through a smart-aleck period, didn't I?
POP: You sure did. Smart-ass period.
RICHARD: I'm over it. I'm gonna be different.
POP: What changed you?
RICHARD: You just change, don't you?
POP: Yeh—you do. And you're changing at a high rate of speed right now, too, ain't you, boy? Horse and me was wondering the other night if it wasn't about time for it. Got hair under your arms yet?
RICHARD (*a beat*): Got it everywhere!

POP: You're gonna be all right, boy!

RICHARD: I want to be like you and Horse, Pop.

POP (*slams a fist on the bar*): Men!

RICHARD (*awkwardly slams a fist on the bar*): Men.

POP: You're off to a good start! Any after what you just told me—now you got a little more going for you—you're not going to miss reading nearly as much as you think you will.

RICHARD: But I won't end up like Horse—with two women. Not me.

POP: Probably not. Not many that lucky.

RICHARD: I wouldn't do that to two women. To either of them. You know what that does to a woman? Even to Faye Precious. To be one of many?

POP: She's one of two.

RICHARD: After awhile she can't help but feel betrayed, let down, whipped, defeated, destroyed . . .

FAYE *gaily opens the front door, popping her head in. She wears her waitress costume. She sees that* RICHARD *has finished stringing wieners across the ceiling.*

FAYE: Oh—it's so festive! Fes—tive! When you give a party, Sonny, you give a party!

RICHARD: I got your song ready, Faye Precious. (*He pulls sheet music from his hip pocket.*)

FAYE: I can't wait! I told Horse just to meet me here tonight—so I'll have time to run home and change—maybe put on something to match the wieners. (*She glances at the wieners hanging overhead.*) If I can come up with something.

RICHARD (*watching* FAYE *as she begins to read the sheet music*): I hope you like it.

FAYE: I'll love it—if it just doesn't have too much of the meat market in it. You know what I mean, that last little song of yours—how did it go?

RICHARD: "Please Be Frank"?

FAYE: I forgot about that one. I was thinking of "My Love

Is On The Block." I sometimes worry about you having to spend so much time in the meat market. It could hinder your career.

RICHARD: But this is a happy birthday song.

FAYE (*reading the sheet music*): Yes. And what a interesting idea making a happy birthday song so sad.

RICHARD: I didn't mean it to be sad. Is it?

FAYE: Well . . . I'm a little depressed. Sadness just has a way of creeping into your work, Sonny.

RICHARD: Don't sing it sad, Faye Precious.

FAYE: Oh, I won't. If I sung your stuff sad, on top of all the sadness in it—"my love is on the block, my heart is at stake"—why people just couldn't bear it. (*She again looks at the sheet music.*)

RICHARD: You don't like it.

FAYE: It's a sweet little song—I just hope it don't set Horse to crying.

RICHARD: He won't cry. It's his forty-first birthday. He didn't die at forty. He'll be happy.

FAYE: He sure don't look forty-one, that dad of yours. Pop, give me and Sonny a couple of Cokes, and then I'll hurry on home. Let me buy, okay?

RICHARD: Thank you.

She sits at a table, RICHARD *joining her. She hums the tune from the sheet music.*

FAYE: I got this already.

RICHARD: How old do you think I look, Faye Precious?

FAYE: I don't know . . . what are you, twelve?

RICHARD: Fourteen.

POP (*serving the Cokes, winking at* FAYE): And all man, if you know what we mean, Faye Precious.

RICHARD (*turning away*): Why did you have to say that?

FAYE: Kindly turn back around here, Sonny Hallen! My goodness, you think I didn't already know that little secret about you? Why, a woman can spot that the minute it happens.

RICHARD: She can? How?

FAYE (*with a wink*): By looking.

RICHARD: Wow—you sure talk frank, Faye Precious.

FAYE: I know it. And I know I shouldn't. But everybody seems to enjoy it so much I hate to cut it out.

RICHARD: I enjoy it, too . . . I like you, Faye Precious.

FAYE: My goodness, what you'll say for a free Coke, Sonny Hallen!

RICHARD: Did you know I used to hate you?

FAYE: You didn't!

RICHARD: I did.

FAYE: Sonny, does your mother still hate me?

RICHARD: Does that matter?

FAYE: Yes! I just hate to be hated!

RICHARD: Me, too, Faye Precious. I'm the same. And Horse hates me.

FAYE: Oh, he doesn't.

RICHARD: I could've said Mama doesn't hate you—but I didn't.

FAYE: Okay—he hates you a little.

RICHARD: I wish we all liked each other.

FAYE: Well, I like you, and I like your mother and I like Horse. And you like me and you like your mother and you like Horse. And your mother likes you . . . and she likes Horse, too . . . And Horse . . . well, he likes me. See—that's a lot of liking.

POP: Crap—I'm going to the toilet!

He exits.

RICHARD: You like Horse a lot, don't you?

FAYE: He's the sweetest man I ever knew.

RICHARD: I wish . . .

FAYE: What?

RICHARD: No.

FAYE: Come on, say it. If it's hard to say it'll just be that much more interesting to hear.

RICHARD: I wish when I grew up . . . I'd seem as sweet to you as Horse does.

FAYE: Why, Sonny . . . you've got my whole body in goose bumps.

RICHARD: I do?

FAYE: Want to feel them?

RICHARD: Sure.

FAYE: Here. Touch. (*She extends an arm.* RICHARD *runs three fingers slowly, gently across her arm. And then again.*) Oh, my, they're getting bigger. (*She retrieves her arm, cradles it.*) Don't you worry about your future. You're gonna be sweetness itself. (*She rises—a little desperate.*) I better be going!

RICHARD: No. Let me buy *you* a Coke now.

FAYE: Oh, no—I know when I've had enough. (*She hurries to the door.*) Bye, bye, sweetness. (*She waves at the door, exits.*)

RICHARD (*crossing to the piano, playing as he sings*):

My love is on the block
And my heart is at stake
Don't chuck my heart away
It's too tender to break.

My love is on the scale
And it's right in its prime
The choice is yours to weigh
Wrap my love while there's time.

You make each encounter so rich and so rare
Just lean on my shoulder and tell me you care.
My life is groundless and grisly and your
Love is the only cure.

My love is on the rack
And it's time to take stock
My heart is on the lam

Take my love off the block
Take my love off the block!

As he finishes the song, he moves downstage to speak with his mother in the audience.

RICHARD: I did fall a little in love with her, Mama. I know I wasn't seeing her the way you did. This is the way I saw her. Can you understand now, Mama? (*He gets only silence from his mother.*) Oh.

He returns upstage as HORSE *staggers through the doorway.* HORSE *carries a bloody apron over his shoulder. He drops it on the bar.*

HORSE: I'm dying! Where is everybody? I went home for help but your mama wasn't there.

RICHARD: You don't usually go home.

HORSE: I'm not usually dying! When I'm dying I go home! She's gotta remember that!

RICHARD: You've already started celebrating?

HORSE: Every salesman remembered me with a bottle—only nobody remembered what I drink! From whisky to gin to rum—and one no-good brought tequila. I hate Mexicans! (*He has staggered to the toilet door, begins to pound on it.*) This is locked!

POP (*shouting through the door*): I'm in here!

HORSE: Well, open up!

POP (*again shouting through the door*): Those who don't drink it here got no right to lose it here!

HORSE: Okay—sell me a beer. I'll lose that for you, too.

Now POP *opens the toilet door.*

POP: One beer—coming up!

HORSE (*exiting hurriedly into the toilet*): Everything coming up!

MARY *enters with a bundle, which she proudly unwraps, revealing a cake box.*

MARY: Isn't he going to be in some shape to eat cake?
RICHARD: You made a cake? For him?
MARY: I did. And then dropped it when I heard him coming in the front door. I barely got out the back door. Why did he come home?
HORSE (*from the toilet*): Pop—you're out of towels!
POP: He went home to die—only he couldn't find you and he refused to do it alone—now he's doing it in my clean toilet! Coming, Horse! (POP *exits into the toilet.*)
RICHARD (*lifting the cake-box lid*): Let me see it.
MARY: It's ruined. The legs flattened out when I dropped it.
RICHARD (*looking into the cake box, but not removing the cake—the audience doesn't see it*): Legs? Oh, Mama—a cake like a meat block! How'd you ever think of that?
MARY: I don't know—it just came to me.
RICHARD: The first one you ever baked him?
MARY: I used to offer. But you don't offer to bake a birthday cake, do you? You just bake it.
RICHARD: I hope he won't drink so much he can't eat it—be too sweet for him.
MARY (*removing a bottle from her purse*): I took care of that.
RICHARD (*seeing the bottle*): Ketchup?
MARY: It's all made of meat.
RICHARD: Oh, Mama—when you do something like this, I know you and Dad could be happy. (*A glance at the mother in the audience.*)
MARY: You worry too much about people being happy.
RICHARD: I don't just worry. I do something. You wait—before this party is over, I'm going to make you and Dad happy. Forever.
MARY: Now that'd be quite a trick.
HORSE (*stomping from the toilet, followed by* POP): Okay, Pop, set me up a beer and we'll get it all going again! (*And then to* MARY.) Where the hell were you? I went home first—figured you'd want to watch if I died!

MARY: I was helping Sonny with the party.

HORSE: What party?

RICHARD: Look around, Dad. You haven't even noticed.

HORSE: I been too close to death to— (*But he has looked up at the wieners—is now squinting at them.*) Hey, what are those? Hanging up there? You know what they look like to me? Know what?

POP: I bet I do, Horse! I bet I know what you're thinking! (*Laughing.*) 'Cause that's always been what wieners made me think of. Are you the same way, Horse?

HORSE: Hell, everybody's that way. Wieners are the best-selling little item I have. (*He laughs.*)

MARY: That's enough, Horse. Richard did this for you—a surprise.

HORSE: Hung up all them for his papa, did he? Boy, what does that mean? Mary, I bet he really did it for you. You always was a big one for wieners!

MARY: Stop it in front of the boy.

HORSE (*crossing to* MARY): What's the trouble—gone already, Mary? Whisper two dirty words in her ear, Pop, and she's hotter than hell. Always has been.

POP: Which two?

HORSE (*whispering into Mary's ear*): Any two! But she has a leaning toward little ones—like—

MARY (*quietly. Enjoying it—but embarrassed in front of the boy*): Shut up, Horse. Damn you.

RICHARD: Don't worry about me—I know as much as anybody in this room.

HORSE: Since when? You don't know nothing about nothing!

RICHARD: I know about sex.

HORSE: Don't you use that word in front of your mother, boy! And you better not know anything! I'm your father and I haven't told you a word. Not a word has passed my mouth! And it's the father tells the son. Right, Pop?

POP: That's the way, Horse. If you want the boy to grow up straight.

HORSE: Straight or dead—that's the choices!

RICHARD: I've already been told. You waited too long to tell me.

HORSE: I waited till I was good and ready. And found the right words! I feel them coming on now. Sit down, boy.

RICHARD: I already know them.

HORSE: Right when I'm ready? You better not! Did you tell him, Mary? Any boy will talk with his mother is just plain dirty. And so's she!

RICHARD: I didn't learn from her. She never told me a word.

HORSE (*glaring at* MARY): She'll talk about anything. She thinks that's part of being educated!

MARY: I was waiting for you, Horse. Since he had the chance to learn from a master.

HORSE: You're mean—but you're right! (*And then turning to* RICHARD.) Who?! Who told you?

RICHARD: I can't say who he is. He swears you to secrecy. He says he holds the world's record. He's told a hundred and twenty-seven kids.

HORSE: What?!

POP: How do you know how many he's told? How do you keep up?

RICHARD: You just pass him on the street and ask him—any day. "Dutch, how many so far?" And he'll shout out the number.

HORSE: Dutch Vogel. (RICHARD *remains silent.* HORSE *suddenly lifts him by the neck, holds him off the floor.*) Dutch Vogel?!

MARY: There's only one Dutch in town.

HORSE (*returning* RICHARD *to the floor*): Yeh—Dutch Vogel!

POP: He's a married man.

HORSE: Damn Germans, they stick their noses into everything! How many you say he's told?

RICHARD: He'll kill me if he finds out I told you.

HORSE: How many?!

RICHARD: A hundred and twenty-seven.

HORSE: There hasn't been a hundred twenty-seven kids in this town! Has there, Pop?

POP: No.

RICHARD: I know that. Sometimes he drives over to Dalhart and Dumas—tells kids over there.

HORSE: Hell—I got a feeling there's something wrong with that man!

POP: My feelings exactly!

HORSE (*staring at* RICHARD): And I also got a feeling any boy picks it up that way—there's something wrong with him, too.

MARY: Well, that just about wrecks the future of Sunray, Dumas and Dalhart, doesn't it?

HORSE: What future? Damn dead towns. A hundred and twenty-seven boomtown bastards, that's what they are! Born of poor fools didn't have the sense to move on when the towns moved on. Towns move on, you know. Why, Sunray is somewhere out in California by now. On the ocean. But dumb fools listen to their dumb wives and sit in these God-forgotten places, trying to pretend they're still towns . . . that Sunray never moved on up to Oklahoma, then over to Colorado. Why, Dalhart's in Alaska now. A salesman told me he saw it up there on his vacation. Gave it my regards, he said. Pop, give me a beer. Damn, I'm depressed!

RICHARD: This should be the happiest night of your life.

HORSE: HAPPY?!

RICHARD: You lived to be forty-one. You didn't die when you were forty—like your father.

HORSE: You think that makes me happy? I'm so ashamed of that fact I could die!

RICHARD: But that's why I planned the party! No telling how many more years you're gonna live now!

HORSE (*roaring*): Well, it just so happens I was only living to be forty—I made no plans for forty-one! I couldn't believe it when today came and I was still here! You look forward to something all your life and then it doesn't happen, and you have to go on . . . you want me to celebrate that?

MARY: You didn't want to die. You wouldn't even take a road trip this year, so afraid a car wreck might get you.

HORSE: I was scared to die, yes! Always have been—I admit it! You butcher as many animals as I have, look 'em in their dead faces, you'd be scared to die, too. But I still *wanted* to die! In memory of him! (*He bursts into sobs.*)

POP: Here's your beer.

HORSE (*hoisting the beer*): In memory of him! Betrayed by all but me! Married to the sorriest woman ever lived!

RICHARD: Was my grandmother sorry?

HORSE: A tramp of the first water! Tell him, Mary—I don't care—tell him what kind of blood he's got in him.

RICHARD: What was wrong with her?

POP: Yeh. I never knew she was a tramp.

MARY: She wasn't.

HORSE: Don't try to defend my mother—just because it's my birthday!

RICHARD: What did she do?

HORSE: She quit him—that's what she did! She quit my papa and married another man. Damn, I do not believe in people quitting people. (*He strikes the table with his fist.*)

MARY: She didn't quit him—he died.

HORSE: It's the same thing—you leave one man and you go to another one! Besides, you're forgettin' the important part, Mary—she married that other bastard on the day of my papa's funeral. (*He is crying loudly now.*)

MARY: You know, I believed that for years. Until we went to visit her just before she died. And she got out the marriage license to Mr. Nunn, her second husband, and showed us the date—cried showing it—one year after Horse's daddy died.

HORSE (*sobbing*): Well, I thought it was the same day! I was still crying about my papa when it happened!

RICHARD: How old were you?

HORSE (*a sob*) : Fourteen!

RICHARD : Just like I am now.

HORSE : Nothing like you are! I loved my papa! I left that whore the night she married the new bastard!

MARY : They had no money. She married again so Horse could stay in school.

HORSE : That's a lie. I knew why she married again! Don't forget, I was fourteen! And if I hadn't been old enough to figure it out, my buddy would of told me anyway. He said it to me, "She wants it again"—that's what he said. "She likes it." You think that didn't just about kill me? My own mother? She liked it? She wanted it again? She couldn't go on living without it? You see, that's the kind of mama I had, boy. And the kind of grandmother you had. What do you think of that?

RICHARD : Is it wrong for women to like it?

HORSE : I'm not talking about women—I'm talking about *mothers!* How would you feel if you found out *your* mother liked it?!

RICHARD *gives* MARY *a quick, inquiring look—she turns slowly away, but we spot a slight smile.* HORSE *notices none of this. The front door opens and* FAYE PRECIOUS *enters, dressed gaily.*

FAYE : Oh, heck—the party's already started!

RICHARD : No, it hasn't—you're right on time. Here every body put on hats and aprons. (*From a box he has removed white butcher hats and aprons.*)

HORSE : Where'd you get clean aprons?

RICHARD (*distributing them*) : I hid them at the first of the week.

HORSE (*during this speech* HORSE *goes for his bloody apron on the bar—shows it to* RICHARD) : That's why we ran out—I been wearing a bloody apron for two days! You know what it does to customers, you wait on them in bloody aprons? They lose respect for you. Plus their appetites!

RICHARD: I only took five.

HORSE: You got no feeling for the meat business—you got to keep their minds off blood as much as possible!

FAYE: He's right, Sonny. A butcher come at me with blood on his apron, I'm finished.

Everyone now stands holding a paper hat and apron.

RICHARD: Well, since I have them, won't you put them on? Please?

FAYE: Sure we will. It's like a costume party, isn't it? What a cute idea, Sonny. How'd you ever think of it? (*She begins to put on her apron and hat.*)

HORSE: Don't mess up one of my aprons, Faye Precious!

FAYE: I'm not going to butcher anything! I told you—the very idea makes me woozy. Don't be so mean, Horse. Put yours on.

HORSE: No!

FAYE: Yes, come on. (*She puts the butcher hat on him.*) Nobody in the world ever looked cuter under a butcher hat than you—forgive me, Mrs. Hallen, but it's true, you know it is. Now stand up, Horse. (*She puts the apron around him.*) Why, you get that white apron on you—well, there never was such a man, was there, Mrs. Hallen?

MARY *stands silent, holding her apron and hat, staring at* HORSE.

RICHARD: Please, Mama, put yours on. (*He begins to help* MARY, *she permits this.*) Come on, Pop, you too!

POP: Will I get a piece of the cake? I seen it over there.

RICHARD: Sure—but first we're going to have the song. Sing it now, Faye Precious.

HORSE: I hate songs! No songs on my birthday!

FAYE: I practiced this song almost one hour and I'm gonna sing it!

MARY: What song, Richard?

RICHARD: I wrote it for Dad's birthday. A surprise.

HORSE: If you got something to say to me, say it—don't sing it!

MARY: And taught it to her—she's going to sing it?

RICHARD (*an awareness of his mother in the audience*): You know how she is, Mama—she loves to sing my songs. If I didn't teach it to her, she'd pick it up first time she heard it anyway.

FAYE: That's true, Mrs. Hallen. That's the way I am. I just pick them up. Did you want to sing it to him?

MARY: You know better.

FAYE: I thought I did—unless things changed overnight. But sometimes they do, Mrs. Hallen. I always hope for the best for you—you know that.

RICHARD (*at the piano*): Ready, Faye Precious?

FAYE: And on key—always! (*But* HORSE *rises with irritation.*) Sit down, Horse—I'm about to sing it.

HORSE: I'm going to the toilet.

FAYE: Not till I've sung, you're not.

HORSE: I got to go!

FAYE: Sit down, cross your legs and shut up! (*She pushes him back into a chair.*) You'd take the happy out of happy anything, Horse!

HORSE *makes a large display of crossing his legs.* RICHARD *plays as* FAYE *sings.*

There's one day in each year
That is yours when it's here
It's the day that belongs to you
And each time it appears
Through a lifetime of years
It's the day that belongs to you.

The people who love you
Will always think of you
Wanting to keep you close by their side
So to whom it concerns
Many happy returns
Of the day that belongs to you—

They all turn to HORSE *for his reaction, but he remains silent, disgusted.*

RICHARD: You did it beautiful, Faye.

FAYE: I just love it, Sonny. I do.

RICHARD: You like it, Mama?

MARY: Very nice. (*But spoken with considerable coolness.*)

HORSE: Hell if it is. It's supposed to be a happy birthday song, ain't it? It don't say happy or birthday. I like the real one better. Sing that one, Faye Precious. (FAYE *glances at* RICHARD.) Go on—sing it!

FAYE: You mind, Richard? It's not as depressing as this one, you keep saying "happy" over and over, you know. I think that's what Horse is missing.

HORSE: That's the one. Sing it!

FAYE:

Happy birthday to you,
Happy birthday to you—

HORSE: Wait a minute! When somebody starts singing that song, everybody else joins in—if they're honest to God celebrating somebody's birthday. That's the way that song is sung! Start over and join in!

FAYE (*a desperate glance at the others for support*): Happy birthday to you. (*Gesturing with her hands to pull them into the song.*)

RICHARD, MARY, POP & FAYE (*as the others join in, they do it with no spirit, no joy. The song ends with a painful flatness*):

Happy birthday to you
Happy birthday, dear Horse
Happy birthday to you.

HORSE (*sniffling*): Now that kind of got me—all of you singing it to me.

MARY: You're cruel—Sonny wrote his song as a birthday present for you.

HORSE: That little song was his birthday present to me? Well, isn't this a lousy party!

RICHARD: Give him your cake, Mama.

POP: Yeh—let's have the cake.

HORSE: I hate cake! You'd like to see me sick all night, wouldn't you, Mary Hallen? That'd be a party for you!

RICHARD: It's not that kind of cake.

He lifts the cake from its box, holds it before HORSE. *This is the first time the audience has seen the cake. There are four legs, now somewhat squashed, under it.*

HORSE: Hell—it's not even a cake. What is it?

FAYE: I get it—a meat block! See the legs, Horse. A cake like a meat block. Why, Mrs. Hallen, you're as clever as Sonny.

HORSE: Yeh—they're both out to get me. Cake'd poison me faster than anything.

RICHARD: Taste it, Dad—it's a different cake. (RICHARD *begins to cut slices.*)

HORSE: Cake's cake. I won't touch it! Another beer, Pop.

FAYE (*taking a piece*): I'll taste it.

POP (*coming from the bar for his piece*): Me, too!

FAYE: Why, that's real unusual—what is that?

MARY (*offering the ketchup*): Have some ketchup, Faye Precious.

HORSE: Ketchup on cake? You trying to kill her, too? Oh, you are mean, Mary Hallen.

FAYE: It's good, Horse, and I bet with ketchup it'll just be wonderful.

POP: It does need ketchup. Strangest cake I ever tasted.

HORSE: You're all crazy—give me a piece! (*He takes a piece, takes a bite.*) Why, what is this? Wait a minute—I know! I'd know this anywhere! It's meat! This is meat! If that ain't the damnedest, stupidest—pass the ketchup, it ain't bad.

RICHARD (*proudly handing him the ketchup*): Here, Dad.

HORSE: Tasty! Damn tasty! This is the first cake I ever been able to eat. First cake anybody could ever eat with beer!

(*He sips the beer.*) That's kind of a invention, ain't it? Did you invent this for me, Mary?

RICHARD: Yes—she did.

HORSE: It's good. Damn good. I can eat all of it.

POP *is reaching for another piece.*

HORSE: Stay out of there, Pop—it's my cake and I'm eating it! (HORSE *takes another piece.*) This is one good idea—a meat cake. I like you people when you come up with good ideas!

RICHARD: I'm full of them—open this, Dad. (*From under a table* RICHARD *removes a large black case.*)

HORSE: Why, what's that?

MARY: What is it, Richard?

FAYE: A birthday present, I bet.

HORSE: From you, boy?

RICHARD: From me and Mama.

MARY: Not from me. I didn't know about it.

RICHARD (*a whisper to* MARY): I couldn't tell you, but it's from you.

MARY: Whose money?

RICHARD: I saved it.

MARY: Then it's from you.

POP: Open it, will you, Horse?

HORSE: Shut up, old man. This is my party and I'll open it soon as I know who it's from. Have you two decided?

MARY: From Richard.

HORSE: Thank you, boy. (*Slowly he opens the case.*) Well, holy hell! Look at this!

POP: Ain't they fancy.

FAYE: They're beautiful, Horse! A whole new set of meat tools. I get a little woozy looking at them, but they're beautiful.

HORSE: Look at that cleaver. (*Examining it proudly.*) That's better than the one I own. Where'd you get the money, boy?

RICHARD: I been saving two years.

MARY: Why, Richard?
HORSE: Why? Because I'm his father and it's my birthday! Right, boy?
RICHARD: Right, Dad!
HORSE: Hell, I'm about to cry.
RICHARD: You haven't even heard it all yet, Dad.
MARY: All what?
RICHARD: I want your old set of tools. I want them for mine. I've decided to be a meat-cutter. Like you. I'm telling you tonight I'm becoming a meat-cutter—like my dad. Forever.
FAYE: Isn't that sweet, Horse?
HORSE: You mean that, boy?
RICHARD: I do.
MARY: That's quite a decision.
RICHARD: It's the one I've made.
HORSE: Who says you'll make a good meat-cutter?
RICHARD: You said I got talent for it.
HORSE: What about your talent for other things?
MARY: Yes!
HORSE: Shut up, Mary. You keep out! (*And then again to* RICHARD.) What about it?
RICHARD: What?
HORSE: You write little songs, don't you?
RICHARD: You don't think they're any good, do you?
HORSE: Well, adding it all up, I'd say you got more talent for meat-cutting than you got for songs—yeh.
RICHARD: Then let me be one.
HORSE (*extending a hand to shake with* RICHARD): You make me proud, boy.
RICHARD (*shaking hands*): That's what I want to do—always.

MARY *turns sharply away.* RICHARD *starts to move to her, but* HORSE *stops him.*

HORSE: I tell you what, boy—let's give that song of mine—my birthday song—another listen. It might grow on me.

You remember that song, "I'm Dreaming of a White Christmas"?

RICHARD: Sure.

HORSE: I didn't give a damn for that song first time I heard it. But they just kept playing the bastard on the radio so much kind of wore you down. Faye Precious, sing it again—wear us down!

FAYE *crosses to* RICHARD, *whispers in his ear that they should speed up the song. They do—considerably.*

FAYE:

There's one day in each year
That is yours when it's here
It's the day that belongs to you
And each time it appears
Through a lifetime of years
It's the day that belongs to you.

The people who love you
Will always think of you
Wanting to keep you close by their side
So to whom it concerns
Many happy returns
Of the day that belongs to you—

A long silence when the song is finished.

RICHARD: It's no "White Christmas," Dad.

FAYE: I sung it the best I could.

MARY: He's just a boy—fourteen. A fourteen-year-old wrote that!

HORSE: Shut up, Mary—he knows bad stuff when he hears it! He ain't the world's greatest meat-cutter but he's not much of a songwriter either. Are you, boy?

RICHARD: No, sir. But it's okay—you won't have to hire me. I didn't mean that. That's not the plan. I plan to work somewhere else. Some other town. (*He turns sharply to* FAYE.) If Faye Precious will go with me?

MARY: Who?
HORSE: Faye Precious?
FAYE: Me?
POP: Well, I'll be damned—like father like son.
RICHARD: No! I want to *marry* Faye Precious.
FAYE: Oh, my God!
MARY (*stunned*): Richard—Richard.
HORSE: What is this, Faye Precious?
FAYE: I don't know, Horse. I do remember touching his hand a little this afternoon—God, I didn't mean to—and I guess he just must have gone to pieces.
RICHARD: I've been planning this for a long time. Will you marry me?
HORSE: Hell, no, she won't marry you! Are you crazy, boy? You're a child—she could be arrested.
FAYE: Could I? Oh, my God—I just touched his hand!
RICHARD: I'm going to marry Faye Precious and take her away with me, and be a meat-cutter and support her, and we'll live in another town, and you can come visit us sometimes and we'll come visit you and Mama sometimes! And that's it!
HORSE: So that's it! Why, you dirty little bastard—you are crazy. Your son's crazy, Mary!
MARY: Of course he is—and you drove him there. He grew up watching you and that . . . that—
HORSE: Watch what you call her!
FAYE: Yeh—watch what you call me!
MARY: WAITRESS! (*And then a nod to* POP, *to confirm what she equates with "waitress."*)
HORSE: Oh, I been too good to you, Mary Hallen—that's my whole trouble! Me and Faye Precious coming in here every night—associating with you and the boy. We didn't have to do that, you know. We could've just gone off and—
FAYE (*clapping her hands to drown out Horse's speech*): Horse, for God's sake, shut your filthy mouth! You already heard what she thinks of me.

HORSE: I don't care. I want her to know the truth about me! I could've been a lot more wicked than I am, Mary! And I should've! Oh, I wanted to be a lot more! I just ached to be more wicked! Lots more than I am!

MARY (*striking* HORSE *hard across the face*): Impossible!

HORSE (*suddenly resorting to a whine like a baby*): Why, you devil! Why did you do that? You never hit me before in your life!

MARY: You've destroyed my son!

RICHARD *stands at the far side of the room—his back to the rest of them—alone, silent.*

HORSE: I haven't touched him—but if he causes a wife to hit her own husband, then it's time to touch him. (*He turns to* RICHARD.) You've ruined my life for . . . (*and then quickly turning to* MARY) How old is he?

MARY: Fourteen.

HORSE: Fourteen years! And I'm going to put an end to it. Now! (*He suddenly picks up the cleaver.*)

MARY: Horse—for pity's sake!

FAYE: Oh, my—I'm getting woozy. Don't swing that thing, Horse.

HORSE (*throwing out his arms for help*): Then somebody hold me down—you know how I am with a cleaver!

FAYE: Pop, hold him down!

POP: Not me! I know how he is with a cleaver!

POP *ducks behind the bar.* HORSE *swings the cleaver again, moving toward* RICHARD.

FAYE: Do something, Mrs. Hallen!

MARY: He wouldn't touch Richard. Wouldn't dare.

FAYE: The hell he wouldn't! I'm woozy as hell, but I'll have to stop him. Stop, Horse! Stop, stop! (*She throws herself between* HORSE *and* RICHARD, *but* HORSE *continues advancing, slowly swinging the cleaver.* FAYE PRECIOUS *sticks a hand into the path of the cleaver, then jerks it back quickly.*) Oh, son of a bitch, Horse, I could just kill you, you damn meat-cutter! Look what you've done to me! (*She holds up an injured finger, but* HORSE *ignores it, continues advancing on* RICHARD. FAYE PRECIOUS *runs to the table, takes the ketchup bottle, pours ketchup up and down her white apron, arms, face, hair, then turns screaming to* HORSE.) Look! Look, Horse! What you've done to me! Turn and look, you damn meat-cutter!

HORSE (*turning, seeing* FAYE): Holy hell—I told you I'm a devil with a cleaver! Faye Precious—what have I done to you? (*He drops to his knees, wraps his arms about Faye's legs.*)

MARY: I will say this for you, Faye Precious—you do have a way with him.

FAYE: Yeh—got him to his knees, don't I, Mrs. Hallen? (*She winks at* MARY, *but then looks down.*) But looking down at all this "blood." Oh, my God, I shouldn't have looked . . . I'm feeling so woozy . . .

HORSE (*holding* FAYE *by the legs, sobbing*): Faye! What have I done?!

FAYE: I'm fainting, Mrs. Hallen—oh, God, I'm fainting. Catch me, Mrs. Hallen—catch me!

And FAYE PRECIOUS *does collapse—into Mary's arms,* HORSE *still holding tightly to her legs.* RICHARD *moves toward the audience.* FAYE, HORSE *and* MARY *freeze in position. The scrim is slowly lowered, but they remain lighted and visible.*

RICHARD (*on the forestage, illuminated by a spotlight*): My plan had been to save your marriage. To get you and him closer together. And that's how close I got you. About as close as I'd ever be able to get you. So—what do you do if you can't join them, Mama?

The spotlight goes out, the stage goes to dark as RICHARD *exits. The house lights come up.*

ACT THREE

The stage is dark, but as RICHARD *enters there is a soft light on him. He is wearing a coat, carrying a suitcase, spinning a 45 rpm record on his finger. He speaks directly to his mother.*

RICHARD: How do you like the idea of me as a songwriter, Mama? How's *that* for disguise? Wait till you see me in this act. I become successful. *At eighteen.* Remember my first trip? The first time I left you and him and her alone? I *was* eighteen—old enough to make a little trip by myself. But were the three of you old enough to be left alone? *I* didn't think so, of course. And so I hurried to get back. (*Hammering begins.*) But before I could get back . . .

The hammering grows louder. He laughs, shrugs, watches as POP *enters from the toilet, then exits. The lights on the stage come up full.*

It is now 1955, and again the bar's decor has been altered. The large photograph of Truman has been replaced by one of Dwight Eisenhower. The faded "Welcome" sign still hangs, but POP *has apparently been the victim of a sign salesman, for now there are cardboard glitter signs placed about prominently. They feature such wit as: IN GOD WE TRUST, EVERYBODY ELSE PAYS CASH; IF YOU CAN READ THIS YOU NEED ANOTHER DRINK; USE YOUR HEAD—IT'S THE LITTLE THINGS THAT COUNT;*

KEEP YOUR TEMPER—NO ONE ELSE WANTS IT; WORK—THE CURSE OF THE DRINKING CLASS.

POP *now stands at the toilet door, staring in. More loud hammering is heard from within. And then Horse's shout.*

HORSE: Finished! Hand me in my toothbrush, Pop!

POP *hands him the toothbrush.* HORSE *disappears in the toilet again.* POP *again stares inside.*

POP: I didn't see your razor before. You going to do your shaving in there, too?
HORSE: I'm going to do my everything in here. That woman has humiliated me for the last go-round!
POP: I don't like you taking over my toilet! That's a public place, you know.
HORSE (*standing in the door—admiring his work*): Who's going to notice a little toothbrush hanging there?
POP: Suppose they use it?
HORSE: Who?
POP: The public.
HORSE: They better damn not!
POP: You better put your name over it—a little sign.
HORSE: And let it get out all over town this is where I brush my teeth now?
POP: You care who knows?
HORSE: Of course I care! I'm ashamed to death of it! What respectable husband wouldn't be?
POP: I told you there'd come a night you'd get home too late.
HORSE: The point is I get home every night. And then to get there and come upon what I did. To see my toothbrush holder nailed outside on the front porch—my razor hanging there by it. Why, that broke my heart! (POP *laughs.*) You think it's funny?
POP: I do.
HORSE: So did Mary. That's when I let her have it.
POP: You hit her?

HORSE: She was doubled over with laughter—I straightened her back up.

POP: You shouldn't of hit her.

HORSE: What about what she done? Nailing my personals to the front porch. Like she expected me to use them out there.

POP: Maybe she did.

HORSE: Sure she did. That was the funny part to her. Well, I showed her! I yanked those devils right from the wall. And told her I was taking them elsewhere—I was taking my personals elsewhere—going to use them elsewhere for the rest of my life. I tell you, Pop, that bothered her a lot more than slugging her did.

Suddenly the front door flies open and FAYE PRECIOUS *races in, wearing her waitress costume. She is carrying a bowl of salad and a knife and fork. She is followed by* MARY, *who wears a black scarf to conceal her right eye.*

FAYE: I don't have nothing! I don't even know what you're talking about!

MARY: You do! You've got it! And I want it back! I'm gonna get it back if I have to search you!

FAYE: I don't have it! Horse, thank God you're here! She came running into the café right at the busy supper hour. (*She slams the bowl of salad and the knife and fork on the bar.*)

MARY: I'll strip you if I have to, Faye Precious.

FAYE: She yelled that right in front of the customers! I could've died. (*A pause—softly.*) Horse, for God's sake, where's your toothbrush?

HORSE: That what you want, Mary? You think she's got it?

MARY: I know she's got it!

FAYE: I ain't got it!

HORSE (*with a snap of the fingers*): Oh, I wish I'd thought to give it to her!

FAYE: But you didn't! Tell her you didn't!

POP: Of course he didn't, Mary.
MARY: Then who? Who's got it?
POP: I got it! I ended up with the whole damn mess. Look in there!

He pulls MARY *to the rest room door. She looks inside, stands staring for a moment, then enters the toilet, returns carrying the toothbrush. She crosses to her table, sits quietly, holding the toothbrush in her hand. They all stare at her. Finally* HORSE *crosses to her.*

HORSE: Happy now?

For an answer MARY *lifts her scarf, reveals her bruised eye, then quickly pulls down the scarf again. But there is time for* FAYE *to see the eye, too.*

FAYE: My goodness, Horse—look at that eye. That was a terrible thing to do to her.
HORSE (*smiling at* MARY): That wasn't the terrible thing I did to her. I've hit her before—but I never moved my personals before. I hope I don't have to do that again. But I tell you what I am doing, Mary Hallen—I'm leaving that toothbrush *holder* nailed up in there . . .
POP: Damn.
HORSE: I can use it any time I get the urge. So watch yourself, Mary Hallen. (*He leans over, speaks directly into her face.*) Watch yourself!

MARY *remains silent.*

POP: I wouldn't push my luck, Horse.
HORSE (*he gestures with an arm in the direction of each woman*): I've been pushing it all my life. Haven't you noticed? (*And he sails from the bar, out the front door.*)

FAYE *moves to* MARY, *but* MARY *continues to sit staring forward. Finally* FAYE *speaks with a touch of envy.*

FAYE: Remember the time Horse hit me?
MARY: He never hit you!

POP: 'Course he didn't.

FAYE: He did too! I got stitches at the back of my head. Want to see the scar? (*She lifts her hair, tries to get* MARY *to look, but* MARY *will not.*)

POP: How come nobody ever heard about it before?

FAYE: We hushed it up. Didn't want anybody to worry about us having troubles, or anything. (*A beat as she turns to* MARY *again.*) We've got lots of things in common, Mary.

MARY: I realize we have a great deal in common, Faye Precious. In fact, I would say there is only one thing we don't have in common.

FAYE (*innocent*): What don't we have in common? Tell me.

But MARY *remains silent, facing forward, daring* FAYE *to figure out what it is.*

POP: She's holding it in her hand! (MARY *still holds tightly to Horse's toothbrush.*) His toothbrush. *She's* got it—and it looks like *she's* gonna keep it.

FAYE: Oh. (*She stares at* MARY, *and then at the toothbrush.*) Well . . . I sure hope you'll be happy with it. (MARY *rises proudly, turns and exits out the front door.* FAYE *shrugs at* POP.) I do. (*Moving to the window, peering after* MARY.) The way she took on, you'd think the toothbrush was close to being the key to marriage.

POP: Don't worry, Faye Precious—you got the key.

FAYE (*not registering Pop's comment, staring out the window*): Uh, oh! Look who's coming up the street. (FAYE *races to the door, opens it, shouts.*) Hurry, Mary—you can hide in the toilet!

MARY (*dashing in*): I don't want him to see my black eye.

FAYE (*a consoling arm about* MARY): 'Course you don't. Duck in the toilet and I'll think fast and come up with something! (*Pushing* MARY *into the toilet.*) Got it already! (*She shuts the toilet door, turns to* POP.) Quick, Pop—take this dollar, go to the drug store, get a pair of sunglasses.

POP: Sunglasses?

The front door opens and RICHARD *enters wearing a light coat and carrying a suitcase.*

FAYE: Well, look who's back! Hi there, sweetheart! Got a kiss for Faye?
RICHARD: Hi, Faye Precious. Sure. (*He puts down his suitcase, crosses to her.*)
FAYE (*whispering to* POP): Go on, Pop—get 'em!
POP: I'm gonna buy them got little stars on the edges.
FAYE: Just hurry!
RICHARD: What you up to, Pop?

POP *pats* RICHARD *on the back as he hurries toward the front door.*

POP: Glad you're back, boy! We sure missed you a lot—and you sure missed a lot! (*And he is gone.*)

FAYE: My kiss, please. (RICHARD *reaches to kiss her, touches the back of her head with his hand.*) Oh—careful of my scar.
RICHARD: Scar?
FAYE: It acts up sometimes.
RICHARD: What scar?
FAYE: Didn't you know about my scar—would you like to see it? (*She bends her neck, parts her hair so that he can see it.*) Twelve stitches.
RICHARD (*staring at the scar*): How did that happen?
FAYE: Horse. Knocked me against the coffee urn at the café. You never knew about that?
RICHARD: No. Why?
FAYE: Oh, it was my fault. I was teasing him about Mrs. Buford Taylor. About that summer night she went crazy and ran naked. Were you old enough to remember that?
RICHARD: No.
FAYE: Somebody spotted her at the edge of town hanging her clothes on the city limit sign. The Sheriff had to form a

posse to catch her. Every man in the county volunteered. Out all night, up and down the hills looking for her. And reports over the radio—men pouring in from Dalhart . . . Dumas, even Amarillo to help out. Mainly degenerates. And Horse leading the pack. Well, about dawn they found her, but then they couldn't find Horse. Didn't find him till almost noon. He'd fallen in a ditch and couldn't get out. That's what I was teasing him about. I said I bet he was in the same ditch with Mrs. Buford Taylor all night. He said he never even got a look at Mrs. Taylor. He was the first man down—and hundreds of men ran right over him looking for her. Well, I just kept on teasing him—"You were in that ditch with Mrs. Buford Taylor." (*And then imitating Horse's voice.*) I wasn't! (*Her own voice.*) You were. (*His.*) I wasn't! (*Hers.*) You were! Till finally he knocked me against the coffee urn.

RICHARD: For what?

FAYE: You know how he is—always banging away at people he loves. Might get you in the back of the head—might be . . . (*a weak laugh*) right in the eye.

RICHARD: Where's Mama, Faye? I called her soon as I got off the bus.

FAYE: Stay gone two months, can't expect people to still be standing where you left them.

RICHARD *turns toward the door.*

RICHARD: Look, Faye, I want to find Mama. I'll be back later. (*He heads for the door.*)

FAYE: No—wait.

RICHARD: Why? (*A beat.*) Something's happened.

FAYE: You know how Horse is—always banging away at people he—

RICHARD: He hit her?

FAYE (*spoken rapidly on top of his line*): Just a light one. (*She gestures with her fist—as if slugging someone lightly.*)

RICHARD: Where is she?

FAYE: First there's something you got to understand, Richard.

RICHARD: What?

FAYE: He took away his toothbrush this time—only she came over here and got it back. You know why? Because she wanted it back! Because she intends to keep it. Forever. Can you understand that, Richard?

RICHARD: Can you, Faye?

FAYE: I'm explaining it to you, ain't I? (*But then she begins to cry.*) You remember that time you asked me to marry you?

RICHARD: Yes.

FAYE: That wasn't the worst idea anybody ever had. If I'd just known enough to take quick advantage of a good offer. It might of just been nice and wonderful. What do you think, honey?

RICHARD (*an awareness of the mother in the audience*): I'm older now, Faye. Maybe it seems a little silly to me now.

FAYE: I guess I'm not any older. It just sounds sweet and beautiful to me.

RICHARD: Did you ever think you'd get to marry him?

FAYE: Horse? I knew her from the beginning too, didn't I? Besides, the way he feels about people quitting people, it never entered my mind. I thought he was Catholic for the longest time. Didn't realize he was just moral.

RICHARD: You *never* thought you and Horse would be together?

FAYE: You asking me if I ever made a plan? The answer's no—never. And the same can be said of Horse. *And* of her. She sat over there with you—and no plan. And me over here with him—and no plan. And him not even wanting a plan. Not a plan among us.

RICHARD: Well, I have. I've got one.

FAYE: I'd love to hear a good plan.

POP (*entering with a small sack*): Got 'em! She'll look like a movie star.

FAYE (*rising*): I'll take them to her.

RICHARD (*also rising*) : She's in there? I want to see her.

FAYE (*taking the package from* POP) : Just a minute! She wants to look right when you see her.

FAYE *exits into the toilet.* RICHARD *turns to* POP.

RICHARD : How bad did Horse hit her?

POP : She kept it hid with a little black handkerchief.

RICHARD (*slamming a fist on the bar*) : I could just kill him when he . . .

POP *slams his fist on the bar, too—smiles consolingly at* RICHARD. *They silently acknowledge a moment similar to this that happened once before. Suddenly the front door opens and* HORSE *stands—proudly holding a beef-steak between his hands.*

HORSE : Finest piece of beefsteak in West Tex— (*But he sees* RICHARD.) Oh . . . my boy's back.

RICHARD : Just in time, I'd say.

HORSE : Better not say much. Better keep that mouth out of my business.

RICHARD : When you start slugging her, it's not just your business any more.

HORSE : What happened between her and me was a little home accident—my business! You come on home and I'll see if I can't fix up a little home accident for you!

POP : Oh, dear God, homes sure do bring out the worst in people.

RICHARD : I'm not coming home any more.

HORSE : Oh, you're not? Moving on, are you? And what's that supposed to do—break your pappy's heart? What are you, eighteen? I'd be ashamed to let anybody know I stayed home as long as you did! Hell, I'd been mailing my mama post cards for four years by the time I was eighteen.

POP : Horse, don't talk to the boy that way—he may be serious about leaving.

HORSE : Hell, he better be—better not be lying to his papa!

I'm all excited about this news. So long, Sonny! You set that one to music and *I'll* sing it!

FAYE (*racing in from the toilet*): Horse, stop it! Think we can't hear you in there? Wall's paper thin and now she's crying again. You get out of—(*She spies the beefsteak.*) Oh—a piece of beefsteak. Now wasn't that thoughtful! You do have a tender side, Horse. (*Taking the steak.*) Ooh—and so does this. But you get on back to the meat market now—so Mary can get herself composured and come out—it's stuffy in there!

HORSE: I was just bidding my boy good-bye—but I can make it quick. GOOD-BYE, BOY! (*And then at the door—as an afterthought.*) For God's sake at least *try* to do a few of the things I done.

He waves a farewell hand, turns and exits proudly. There is a moment's silence, then FAYE *turns to* RICHARD.

FAYE: You're not really leaving, are you?

MARY *suddenly enters from the toilet, wearing the sunglasses.*

MARY: Of course he is! (*She moves directly to the piano, begins to play and sing.* POP *goes into the toilet the moment* MARY *enters.*)

Free
Ev'ryone wants to be free
Free from a lock and a key
Ev'ryone—

FAYE & MARY (FAYE *smiles, joins* MARY *in singing*):

Including me
Flight
Ev'ryone wants to take flight
Flight from their fears in the night
Ev'ryone
Including me

Beyond the rocks
Out where it's calm and serene
Out where no breakers are seen
That's where I long to roam—

RICHARD: How did you learn that? You've never seen that song.

MARY: Let us finish. Don't you like the way we're doing it?

RICHARD: How did you get it?

FAYE (*she points to the jukebox*): By listening and listening.

RICHARD: They got a record here already? How? I was bringing one home in my suitcase.

FAYE: The man owns the juke brought it in day before yesterday. He was excited as us. First time it's ever happened in his territory.

RICHARD: I didn't figure they'd send them out before I got back. I have one in my suitcase just for you, Mama. To put on our player.

MARY: I've already heard it several times.

RICHARD: Damn, I wanted to be here when you heard it!

MARY: If you'd told me what you were up to, I'd waited.

RICHARD: I wasn't ready to tell yet—because I wasn't sure it'd come true. But it has! And now I got a plan! Wait till you hear it

MARY: I already know it . . . Let's finish the song, Faye. I like the way we sing it.

FAYE & MARY:

Just drifting on and on
Beneath a sapphire crown
And oh, so happy to be where
The sun doesn't ever go down.

During the song, RICHARD *crosses downstage, stares out at the mother in the audience.*

Beyond the rocks
Out where a heartache can cease
Out where there's nothing but peace.

MARY *silences* FAYE *with a touch of the hand, finishes the song alone.*

MARY:

That's where *he* longs to roam
And he'd never
No never
Come home.

(*A beat—and then she speaks.*) Your plan.

FAYE: Is that it? You really going to leave us, Sonny?

RICHARD: That's just part of it. I want you to come with me.

FAYE: Who?

RICHARD: My mother.

FAYE: Oh.

RICHARD: That's the whole plan. You're not going to believe the money I'll have—they like six more of my songs and all my ideas. I'll take you anywhere you want to go.

FAYE: Go? Where does she want to go? You don't like to travel, do you, Mary

MARY: When did you start calling me Mary?

FAYE: Oh—sometime this afternoon. I guess.

RICHARD: This is between her and me, Faye Precious. You're leaving Horse and Faye Precious—let them have what they want!

FAYE: And what in the world do we want? Would you tell me that one?

RICHARD: Each other.

FAYE: You got a way of putting things that's disgusting! You're not about to leave here, are you . . . Mrs. Hallen?

MARY: You don't want to be left with him?

FAYE: Why, you got a streak in you like your boy's, don't you? (*She begins to cry.*) What have I ever done to you people?

RICHARD: You don't want him?

FAYE: Want him? I don't understand any of this! I love him like all the rest of you, that's all. What's happening to everybody all of a sudden?

RICHARD: Maybe we don't love him so much.
FAYE: You do, too! Don't you, Mrs. Hallen?
MARY: I'm not so sure, Faye Precious.
FAYE: Oh, don't say that! Don't you see what this is? Don't you see? Your boy's in love with me! Yes! Has been for years. Will we ever forget that night he tried to get me to marry him? Well, he can't have me! (*She stands proudly.*) I've made that so clear. And now, to get revenge on his daddy—who does have me—he wants to take you away. It's revenge, Mrs. Hallen. Revenge over his lust for me! But I'm not going to let it happen. Because I know who to tell! And if you don't think he'll come right back over here—and he won't be carrying a steak this time! And you know what I mean! And another thing! This is one time Faye Precious will not raise her already sliced finger to save you!

She raises her already sliced finger, then turns and runs from the bar. RICHARD *stares silently at* MARY.

RICHARD: Mama, I didn't go to Dallas. I went all the way to Nashville, Tennessee. That's where they made my record. Mama, I want you to come with me. Back to Nashville. It's a good place to live. We're going to pack your suitcase right now. The bus is due in twenty minutes. (MARY *turns silently away.*) Mama, you don't know how it's hurt me all these years—watching all this.
MARY: You think it hasn't hurt me? It killed me to have you see. (*A beat.*) I left him once—took you and left him.
RICHARD: You never left him.
MARY: Once. You weren't three. We took the bus out. But it hadn't got ten miles when I spotted his old pickup out the rear window—following. Another mile and he'd caught up with us and run that bus right off the road into a ditch. Three passengers were injured. I said I could've been injured. But he said, "Hell, I knew which side to run it off the road on—I knew which side you were sitting on, Mary."

RICHARD: You wanted him to run it off the road.

MARY: I was headed back home to mama and papa. Back to *East* Texas. Where there is nobody in the world who'd run a bus off a road for you. Much less have the good sense to run it off on the proper side. (*A beat.*) And allow me to come climbing out safely. And back to him.

RICHARD: For how long?

MARY: A night. Which can be enough.

RICHARD: I want better than that for you, Mama. A lot better. I want to show you what it's like when somebody really cares about you. You've never known it. Let me show you. I love you, Mama. (*He drops to his knees beside her, glances at his mother in the audience.*)

HORSE (*pushing the front door open*): I heard that! I heard it! Right outside this door! It came through the door! (*Pointing to* RICHARD, *still on his knees.*) Look at him there—on his knees! Oh, I had my eyes on the two of you for years! I want the truth, and I want it fast! You and her going away together? Is that your plan?

RICHARD: That's it.

HORSE: Well, if that don't beat any plan of man or beast! That's the filthiest, dirtiest thing I ever heard of! My own wife and my own boy running off together! Son of a bitch!

FAYE: I told you, Horse.

HORSE: I know you did. Son of a bitch! (*And then turning to* MARY.) Mary—what have you got to say for yourself?

MARY: The boy wants me to live with him, Horse.

HORSE: Shut your dirty mouth, Mary! Don't speak it no plainer than I already spoke it.

RICHARD (*suddenly moving to his suitcase*): Come on, Mama. I'll help you pack. We can have the rest of your things shipped.

FAYE: Don't count on me to help ship anything, Mrs. Hallen. I won't do it.

RICHARD: Then she can do without them. She'll have new things. And nice ones.

HORSE *grabs* RICHARD *violently by the throat, throws him across a table. The boy's head and legs hang off the table.* HORSE *suddenly sits astride of him.*

HORSE: Look, you—I've had it with you!
MARY: Leave the boy alone.
HORSE (*continuing to hold* RICHARD *by the neck, turning sharply to* MARY): Then you tell him good-bye forever! Say good-bye to your boy! (*Tightening his grip on Richard's neck.*) Tell him! So long, Sonny!
MARY: You won't hurt him!
HORSE: I'll kill him!

RICHARD *makes a groaning sound as* HORSE *continues to hold him tightly.*

MARY: Let him go, Horse!
HORSE: If he'll go by himself! That's the only way! (*He loosens his hands from Richard's throat for a moment.*) Will you?
RICHARD (*winded but loud*): No!!
HORSE (*tightening his hands about* RICHARD *again*): Okay—good-bye to my only son!
FAYE: My God, Mrs. Hallen—do something! I don't want to watch the boy die right here!
POP: Hell, I never thought I'd have to invent a rule about killing in here. No dancing or killing, Horse!

HORSE *continues his grip on Richard's throat. There are desperate groans from* RICHARD *now.*

MARY (*finally a shout*): I won't go, Horse!
HORSE (*still strangling* RICHARD): Never? Say never, Mary! You'll never go! (*There is a pause*—MARY *hesitates.*) You better say it fast—the boy's dying right here in my hands!
MARY (*from deep within herself*): I'll never go, Horse! Never! Never!

HORSE (*still strangling* RICHARD) : Thank you, Mary. Thank you. My marriage is saved.

FAYE : Let go of the boy, Horse.

HORSE (*releasing* RICHARD) : Sure. Sure. (RICHARD *is gagging.* HORSE *slaps him on the back.*) You'll be all right in a minute, boy. Just get your breath, your papa's got a grip like a bull, you got to remember that. Okay now?

RICHARD (*still gasping for breath, looking up at* HORSE) : Why do you want her to stay?

FAYE : Sonny, *when* is your bus due to leave?

RICHARD : Why do you want her?

HORSE : Don't make your last words to me smart ass, boy. Don't do it!

RICHARD (*a plea*) : Why?

HORSE : Because she's my wife—that's why. I was the first man ever took that little innocent virgin to bed and I'm going to be the last man takes her to bed. Because that's marriage! (*He points at* MARY.) That woman there has stayed within the bounds of marriage and she's going to continue staying there, difficult as it is! She is no whore! She's better than my own mama. She's the only thing in my life that's . . . that's so good I could . . . I could show her to God, if I wanted to! And you're not taking that away from me—nor anybody else! She's my fine thing, damn you. My fine thing! (*He sits at the table, puts his head in his hands, begins to cry.*)

FAYE : I always said he thought awful highly of you, Mrs. Hallen. Don't cry, Horse—please. That was so sweet. Wasn't it, Mrs. Hallen?

But MARY *only stares at* HORSE. RICHARD *crosses silently to his suitcase, picks it up.*

MARY : You really going?

RICHARD : What can I do here?

FAYE (*turning sharply to him*) : Nothing! It's all been done—a long time ago.

MARY : You can kiss me good-bye.

HORSE *lifts his head from the table, watching as* RICHARD *moves to* MARY. *She opens her arms to embrace him.*

HORSE: Just good-bye!

MARY *and* RICHARD *kiss briefly and then he again turns to exit.*

MARY: Say something to him, Horse—please.
HORSE: What?
MARY: Something!
HORSE: Boy!
RICHARD (*pausing—turning to* HORSE): Yes.
HORSE: How the hell you going to make a living? You're no first-class meat-cutter, you know that?
RICHARD: On my songs.
HORSE: I heard that one in there. (*He points to the jukebox.*) You going to make a living from them?
RICHARD: Yes.
HORSE: How? You trying to tell me every time I pop a nickel in there it goes to you?
RICHARD: Part of it. Something like that. I think.
HORSE: You gonna have to live on my nickels?
RICHARD: Yes, sir.
HORSE: Well, don't say your papa never gave you a helping hand. (*He crosses to the jukebox, reaches for a nickel, slams it into the machine. They stand staring at each other as the song begins. It is "Beyond the Rocks," the song* FAYE PRECIOUS *and* MARY *sang earlier in the act, but it has been recorded by a rock and roll group.*) It's got a nice little beat to it, boy!
RICHARD: Yes, sir.
HORSE: Sets my feet going. I feel like dancing. (*He moves toward* FAYE PRECIOUS.)
RICHARD (*quickly setting down his suitcase, reaching* FAYE PRECIOUS *first*): So do I. Faye Precious—a farewell dance?

FAYE *glances at* HORSE, *but then moves to* RICHARD.

FAYE: Sure, honey. But don't miss that bus.
HORSE (*a flash of anger*): Pop—I thought you always said there was no dancing in this place!
POP: I'm an old man. I can't enforce all the rules. I'm going to concentrate on no killing.

HORSE *glares angrily at* FAYE PRECIOUS *and* RICHARD *for another moment as they dance. Then suddenly he turns to* MARY.

HORSE: Can you dance, Mary?
MARY: As well as you can, Horse.
HORSE: I hope that's true! (*He grabs her roughly by the waist, begins to swing her about the floor. They quickly pass* FAYE *and* RICHARD. HORSE *shouts at* RICHARD.) How's this for dancing, boy?
RICHARD: It's fine, Papa. It's wonderful.
HORSE: You bet it is! Mary's as good a dancer as I am, by God!

HORSE *continues to swing* MARY *about the floor.* RICHARD *and* FAYE *cease to dance, he seats her at the table, kisses her lightly on the cheek, picks up the suitcase and moves to the front door. From there he waves to her and to* POP. MARY *and* HORSE *are unaware as they continue dancing.* RICHARD *turns, now watching as the playwright.* FAYE *leans back in her chair, watches* HORSE *and* MARY, *beams with genuine happiness, patting her foot, clapping her hands.* MARY *lets down her long hair, continuing to dance with* HORSE. *The hair flows freely. So does* MARY. RICHARD *puts down his suitcase. The music from the jukebox becomes softer, Horse's dancing less wild, as the scrim is slowly lowered.* RICHARD *speaks directly into the second row.*

RICHARD: I couldn't end it the way it really happened. I couldn't. The stuff about me catching you still doing his laundry—even after he moved in with her. I wrote it like that. But when we got it on stage . . . it just wouldn't work. It didn't seem right. (*A pause.*) It wasn't right, Mama. God, I'm sorry I did it. I should never have made you quit him!

The woman seated in the audience suddenly rises, steps toward the stage, pauses to stare up at RICHARD, *then turns and moves to the rear exit.* RICHARD *stares after her, mouths the word "Mama" silently, then turns, stares at* HORSE *and* MARY. *They continue to dance.* HORSE *runs his fingers through Mary's long hair. After another moment of this the lights fade to dark.*

The Indian Wants the Bronx

Israel Horovitz

There is no crime greater,
more worthy of punishment,
than being strange and
frightened among the strange
and frightened . . . except
assimilation to the end of
becoming strange and
frightened, but apart from
one's own real self.

ISRAEL HOROVITZ

The Indian Wants the Bronx was the first staged reading performed at the Eugene O'Neill Playwrights' Conference in 1966. Two years later it was produced Off-Broadway after having been read and rejected, according to the author, by fifty producers. The play was one of the season's most critically acclaimed dramas. Horovitz received both the Vernon Rice and Obie Awards for distinguished playwrighting.

One-act plays are the Lorelei of drama. The seductive lure of brevity and focus betrays the contrivance and strained emotional epiphany. But when experience is not served up like watercress sandwiches, when emotion can develop as naturally and fully as life itself, there is dignity and genuine force to these cameos. *The Indian Wants the Bronx* is an example of the genre working with ambitious force. Within the framework of a situation, Horovitz finds an irony, a delight in vernacular, which gives the play a gusto and uncovers a new theatrical voice beginning to find its frequency.

The Indian Wants the Bronx isolates a gruesome humor in the randomness of city violence. As a consequence, the play adds another dimension to its terror and strange sadness. New York audiences, like the theater's established reviewers, shy from violence on stage as they turn their backs on life. Horovitz is not so squeamish.

The two city toughs—Murph and Joey—come upon an East Indian waiting for a bus. It is late at night. He speaks no English and is passive, uncertain, and afraid. He shrinks into the shadows as the kids harmonize. They stop occasionally to call across the street to the apartment of their social worker, shouting "Hey, Pussyface." They are loose, playful, afraid of the very response they long for. Their skittish strength and their own fear breed a menace which lurks over their laughter like a low growl. The idiom and the threat are familiar:

MURPH: You're a Turkie-lover, right?
JOEY: Right.
MURPH: Say it.
JOEY: I'm a Turkie-lover.
MURPH: You're a Turkie-humper, right?
JOEY: *You're* a Turkie-humper.
MURPH: Say, *I'm* a Turkie-humper.
JOEY: That's what I said. You're a Turkie-humper. (MURPH *twists his arms a bit further.*) Oww, ya dirty bastard! All right, I'm a Turkie-humper. Now, leggo. (JOEY *pretends to laugh.*)
MURPH: You gonna hug him and kiss him and love him up like a mother?
JOEY: Whose mother?
MURPH: Your mother. She humps Turkies, right?
JOEY: Owwww! All right. Yeah. She humps Turkies. Now leggo!
MURPH (*lets go*): You're free.

When they discover the Indian, they toy with him, laughing at his inarticulateness to forget their own. "Why did you rape all those innocent women and children?"

The game goes on and, in their boredom, they yap around the Indian like nervous dogs. They poke each other, swinging open-fisted and with hair suddenly flapping, like bantam cocks.

Their battles for supremacy, the gouging, the twisting, the adolescent grasping is evocative of Horovitz's vision for laughter and drama: man's need for response and his inadequate equipment to elicit that affection. Murph and Joey have no language of love, no way of connecting. Their "noogies" are a means of testing their strength and of feeling a contact with humanity.

The New York production benefited from the talent which had been lavished on Horovitz's plays at the O'Neill Playwrighting Conference; not only did Horovitz find a director who could control the humor and pain of the horrific, but an actor who would make the role of Murph an Obie Award-winning performance. James Hammerstein, who directed *It's Called The Sugar Plum* at the Conference in 1967, managed to present Horovitz's work with a sense of the body's limitation which the situation demands. His editorial control of both plays which composed the Off-Broadway evening seemed strong, where playing for laughs or straining for high-pitched emotion would be a lesser director's easy out. Al Pacino, who appeared in the original O'Neill staged reading, added a special dimension to Horovitz's play. As a New York tough, a swarthy shadow of the streets, Pacino's movement isolated a frozen truth of the city. His diction was no stylized Brando imitation ("I coulda been a contenda") but something more insanely true: "Bust your squash"; or backhanding the Indian: "How's your teabags?" Pacino, chewing his gum loudly and stretching it over his molars, repeating: "terrific, huh, terrific," shuffling on the balls of his feet, talking while his hands caress his thighs or solar plexus, evokes the brutal past and hopeless future in a body which feels its own confusing strength. There was nothing wasted in his portrayal, there was not a false note. The performance helped Horovitz's script to uncover that most careful thread of its insight—that violence partakes equally of ignorance and fear.

The Indian Wants the Bronx was presented by Ruth Newton Productions on January 17, 1968, at the Astor Place Theatre, New York City, with the following cast:

GUPTA, an East Indian	John Cazale
MURPH	Al Pacino
JOEY	Matthew Cowles

Directed by James Hammerstein

Prior to its New York opening, *The Indian Wants the Bronx* was presented as a work-in-progress at The Loft Workshop, New York; The Eugene O'Neill Memorial Theatre Foundation, Connecticut; Canoe Place Cabaret Theatre, New York; and The Act IV Café Theatre, Massachusetts.

CHARACTERS

GUPTA

MURPH

JOEY

PLACE: *A bus stop on upper Fifth Avenue in New York City.*
TIME: *A chilly September's night.*

As the curtains open the lights fade up, revealing GUPTA, *an East Indian. He is standing alone, right of center stage, near a bus stop sign. An outdoor telephone booth is to his left; several city-owned litter baskets are to his right.*

GUPTA *is in his early fifties. Although he is swarthy in complexion, he is anything but sinister. He is, in fact, meek and visibly frightened by the city.*

He is dressed in traditional East Indian garb, appropriately for mid-September.

As GUPTA *strains to look for a bus on the horizon, the voices of two boys can be heard in the distance, singing. They sing a rock-'n'-roll song, flatly, trying to harmonize.*

FIRST BOY:

I walk the lonely streets at night,
A 'lookin' for your door,
I look and look and look and look,
But, baby, you don't care.
Baby, you don't care.
Baby, no one cares.

SECOND BOY (*interrupting*) : Wait a minute, Joey. I'll take the harmony. Listen. (*Singing.*)
But, baby, you don't care.
Baby, you don't care.
Baby, no one cares.

(*Confident that he has fully captured the correct harmony, boasting.*) See? I've got a knack for harmony. You take the low part.

BOYS (*singing together*) :
I walk . . . the lonely, lonely street . . .
A 'listenin' for your heartbeat,
Listening for your love.
But, baby, you don't care.
Baby, you don't care.
Baby, no one cares.

They appear on stage, FIRST BOY *is* JOEY. SECOND BOY *is* MURPH. JOEY *is slight, baby-faced, in his early twenties.* MURPH *is stronger, long-haired, the same age.*

MURPH (*singing*) :
The lonely, lonely streets, called out for lovin',
But there was no one to love . . .
'Cause, baby, you don't care . . .

JOEY (*joins in the singing*) :
Baby, you don't care . . .

JOEY AND MURPH (*singing together*) :
Baby, you don't care.
Baby, you don't care.
Baby, no one cares.
Baby, no one cares.

MURPH (*calls out into the audience, to the back row: across to the row of apartment houses opposite the park*) : Hey, Pussyface! Can you hear your babies singing? Pussyface. We're calling you.

JOEY (*joins in*) : Pussyface. Your babies are serenading your loveliness.

They laugh.

MURPH: Baby, no one cares.

MURPH AND JOEY (*singing together*):

Baby, no one cares.
Baby, no one cares.

MURPH (*screams*): Pussyface, you don't care, you Goddamned idiot! (*Notices* THE INDIAN.) Hey, Look at the Turk.

JOEY *stares at* THE INDIAN *for a moment, then replies.*

JOEY: Just another pretty face. Besides. That's no Turk. It's an Indian.

MURPH (*continues to sing*):

Baby, no one cares.
(*Dances to his song, strutting in The Indian's direction. He then turns back to* JOEY *during the completion of his stanza and feigns a boxing match.*)
I walk the lonely, lonely streets,
A callin' out for loving,
But, baby, you don't give a Christ for
Nothin' . . . not for nothin'.
(*Pretends to swing a punch at* JOEY, *who backs off laughing.*) You're nuts. It's a Turk!

JOEY: Bet you a ten spot. It's an Indian.

MURPH: It's a Turk, schmuck. Look at his fancy hat. Indians don't wear fancy hats. (*Calls across the street, again.*) Hey, Pussyface. Joey thinks we got an Indian. (*Back to* JOEY.) Give me a cigarette.

JOEY: You owe me a pack already, Murphy.

MURPH: So I owe you a pack. Give me a cigarette.

JOEY: Say "please," maybe?

MURPH: Say "I'll bust your squash if you don't give me a cigarette!"

JOEY: One butt, one noogie.

MURPH: First the butt.

JOEY: You're a Jap, Murphy.

As JOEY *extends the pack,* MURPH *grabs it.*

MURPH: You lost your chance, baby. (*To the apartment block:*) Pussyface! Joey lost his chance!

JOEY: We made a deal. A deal's a deal. You're a Jap, Murphy. A rotten Jap. (*To the apartment:*) Pussyface, listen to me! Murphy's a rotten Jap and just Japped my whole pack. That's unethical, Pussyface. He owes me noogies, too!

MURPH: Now I'll give you twenty noogies, so we'll be even.

He raps JOEY *on the arm.* THE INDIAN *looks up as* JOEY *squeals.*

JOEY: Hey. The Indian's watching.

MURPH (*raps* JOEY *sharply again on the arm*): Indian's a Turkie.

JOEY (*grabs Murph's arm and twists it behind his back*): Gimme my pack and it's an Indian, right?

MURPH: I'll give you your head in a minute, jerkoff.

JOEY: Indian? Indian? Say, Indian!

MURPH: Turkie? Turkie?

JOEY: Turkie. Okay. Let go. (MURPH *lets him up and laughs.* JOEY *jumps up and screams:*) Indian! (*Runs a few steps.*) Indian!

MURPH (*laughing*): If your old lady would have you on Thanksgiving you'd know what a turkey was, ya' jerk. (*Hits him on the arm again.*) Here's another noogie, Turkie-head!

THE INDIAN *coughs.*

JOEY: Hey, look. He likes us. Shall I wink?

MURPH: You sexy beast, you'd wink at anything in pants.

JOEY: Come on. Do I look like a Murphy?

MURPH (*grabs* JOEY *and twists both of his arms*): Take that back.

JOEY: Aw! Ya' bastard. I take it back.

MURPH: You're a Turkie-lover, right?

JOEY: Right.

MURPH: Say it.

JOEY: I'm a Turkie-lover.

MURPH: You're a Turkie-humper, right?

JOEY: *You're* a Turkie-humper.

MURPH: Say, *I'm* a Turkie-humper.

JOEY: That's what I said. You're a Turkie-humper. (MURPH *twists his arms a bit further.*) Oww, ya' dirty bastard! All right, I'm a Turkie-humper! Now, leggo! (JOEY *pretends to laugh.*)

MURPH: You gonna hug him and kiss him and love him up like a mother?

JOEY: Whose mother?

MURPH: Your mother. She humps Turkies, right?

JOEY: Owww! All right. Yeah. She humps Turkies. Now leggo!

MURPH (*lets go*): You're free.

JOEY (*breaks. Changes the game*): Where's the bus?

MURPH: Up your mother.

JOEY: My old lady's gonna kill me. It must be late as hell.

MURPH: So why don't you move out?

JOEY: Where to?

MURPH: Maybe we'll get our own place. Yeah. How about that, Joey?

JOEY: Yeah, sure. I move out on her and she starves. You know that.

MURPH: Let her starve, the Turkie-humper.

JOEY (*hits* MURPH *on the arm and laughs*): That's my mother you're desecrating, you nasty bastard.

MURPH: How do you desecrate a whore? Call her a lady?

JOEY: Why don't you ask *your* mother?

MURPH (*hits* JOEY *on the arm*): Big mouth, huh?

JOEY: Hey! Why don't you pick on som'body your own size, like Turkie, there.

MURPH: Leave Turkie out of this. He's got six elephants in his pocket, probably.

JOEY (*laughs at the possibility*): Hey, Turkie, you got six elephants in your pocket?

MURPH: Hey, shut up, Joey. (*Glances in The Indian's direction and* THE INDIAN *glances back.*) Shut up.
JOEY: Ask him for a match.
MURPH: You ask him.
JOEY: You got the butts.
MURPH: Naw.
JOEY: Chicken. Want some seeds to chew on?
MURPH: I'll give you somethin' to chew on.
JOEY: Go on, ask him. I ain't never heard an Indian talk Turkie-talk.
MURPH: He's a Turkie, I told ya'. Any jerk can see that he's a definite Turk!
JOEY: You're a definite jerk, then. 'Cause I see a definite Indian!
MURPH: I'll show you. (*Walks toward* THE INDIAN *slowly, taking a full minute to cross the stage. He slithers from side to side and goes through pantomime of looking for matches.*)
JOEY: Hey, Murph. You comin' for dinner? We're havin' turkey tonight! Hey! Tell your Turkie to bring his elephants.
MURPH: Schmuck! How's he going to fit six elephants in a rickshaw?
JOEY (*flatly*): Four in front. Three in back.

He reaches THE INDIAN.

MURPH: Excuse me. May I borrow a match?
INDIAN (*speaking in Hindi*): Mai toom-haree bo-lee nrh-hee bol sak-tah. Mai tum-hah-ree bah-sha nah-hee sah-maj-tah. [I cannot speak your language. I don't understand.]
MURPH (*to* JOEY, *does a terrific "take," then speaks, incredulous*): He's got to be kidding.

JOEY *and* MURPH *laugh.*

INDIAN: Moo-jhay mahaf kar-nah mai toom-hah-ree bah-art nah-hee sah-maj sak-tah. [I'm sorry. I don't understand you.]

MURPH: No speak English, huh? (THE INDIAN *looks at him blankly. Louder.*) You can't speak English, huh?

THE INDIAN *stares at him, confused by the increase in volume.*

JOEY (*flatly*): Son of a bitch. Hey, Murph. Guess what? Your Turkie only speaks Indian.

MURPH (*moves in closer, examining* THE INDIAN): Say something in Indian, big mouth.

JOEY (*holds up his hand*): How's your teepee? (THE INDIAN *stares at him. He laughs.*) See.

THE INDIAN *welcomes Joey's laugh and smiles. He takes their hands and "shakes" them.*

MURPH (*catches on as to why* THE INDIAN *has joined the smile and feigns a stronger smile until they all laugh aloud.* MURPH *cuts off the laughter as he shakes The Indian's hand and says*): You're a fairy, right?

INDIAN (*smiles harder than before*): Mai toom-haree bah-at nah-hee sah-maj-tah. Mai ap-nay lah-kay kah gha-r dhoo-nd rah-haw hooh. Oos-nay moo-jhay mil-nah tar pahr nah-jah-nay woh cah-hah hai. Mai oos-kah mah-kan dhoo-nd rah-hah hoon. Oos-kah pah-tah yeh rah-hah k-yah. [I don't understand you. I'm looking for my son's home. We were supposed to meet, but I could not find him. I'm looking for his home. This is his address. Am I headed in the correct direction?] (THE INDIAN *produces a slip of paper with an address typed on it. And a photograph.*)

MURPH: Gupta. In the Bronx. Big deal. (*To* THE INDIAN:) Indian, right? You an Indian, Indian? (*Shakes his head up and down, smiling.* THE INDIAN *smiles, confused.*) He don't know. (*Pauses, studies the picture, smiles.*) This picture must be his kid. Looks like you, Joe.

JOEY: (*looks at the picture*): Looks Irish to me. (*He hands the picture to* MURPH.)

BOTH: Ohhh.

MURPH: Yeah. Why'd you rape all those innocent children? (*Pause.*) I think he's the wrong kind of Indian. (*To* THE INDIAN:) You work in a restaurant? (*Pauses. Speaks with a homosexual's sibilant "s".*) It's such a shame to kill these Indians. They do such superb beaded work. (MURPH *shakes his head up and down again, smiling.*)

INDIAN: (*follows Murph's cue*): Mai-nay ap-nay lar-kay koh su-bah say nah-hee day-kha. Toom-hara shah-har bah-hoot hee barah hai. [I haven't seen my son all day. Your city is so big and so busy.]

JOEY: Ask him to show you his elephants.

MURPH: You ask. You're the one who speaks Turkie-Indian.

JOEY: White man fork with tongue. Right? (THE INDIAN *stares at him blankly.*) Naw, he don't understand me. You ask. You got the right kind of accent. All you foreigners understand each other good.

MURPH: You want another noogie?

JOEY: Maybe Turkie wants a noogie or six?

MURPH (*shaking his head*): You want a noogie, friend?

INDIAN (*agrees*): Moo-jhay mahaf kar-nah. Moo-jay. Yah-han aye zyah-da sah-may na-hee hoo-ah. [I'm sorry. I haven't been here long.]

MURPH: Give him his noogie.

JOEY: Naw. He's your friend. You give it to him. That's what friends are for.

MURPH (*looks at the paper and photograph, gives them back*): Jesus, look at that for a face.

JOEY: Don't make it.

MURPH: Don't make it. Prem Gupta. In the Bronx. Jesus, this is terrific. The Indian wants the Bronx.

JOEY (*sits on a trash can*): He ain't gonna find no Bronx on this bus.

MURPH: Old Indian, pal. You ain't going to find the Bronx on this bus, unless they changed commissioners again. Now I've got a terrific idea for fun and profit. (*Pauses.*)

INDIAN: K-yah kah-ha toom-nay? [Excuse me?]

MURPH: Right. Now why don't you come home and meet my

mother? Or maybe you'd like to meet Pussyface, huh? (*To* JOEY:) Should we bring him over to Pussyface?

JOEY: He don't even know who Pussyface is. You can't just go getting Indians blind dates without giving him a breakdown.

MURPH: Okay, Chief. Here's the breakdown on Pussyface. She's a pig. She lives right over there. See that pretty building? (*Points over the audience to the back row of seats.*) That one. The fancy one. That's Pussyface's hideaway. She's our social worker.

JOEY: That's right.

MURPH: Pussyface got assigned to us when we were tykers, right, Joe?

JOEY: Just little fellers.

MURPH: Pussyface was sent to us by the city. To watch over us. And care for us. And love us like a mother. Not because she wanted to. Because we were bad boys. We stole a car.

JOEY: We stole two cars.

MURPH: We stole two cars. And we knifed a kid.

JOEY: You knifed a kid.

MURPH (*to* JOEY): Tell it to the judge, Fella! (*He takes a pocketknife from his pocket and shows it to* THE INDIAN, *who pulls back in fear.*)

JOEY: The Chief thinks you're going to cut him up into a totem pole.

MURPH: Easy, Chief. I've never cut up an Indian in my life.

JOEY: You've never *seen* an Indian in your life.

MURPH: Anyway, you got a choice. My mother—who happens to have a terrific personality. Or Pussyface, our beloved social lady.

JOEY: Where's the bus?

MURPH: It's coming.

JOEY: So's Christmas.

MURPH: Hey. Show Turkie my Christmas card for Pussyface. (*To* THE INDIAN:) Pussyface gives us fun projects. I had to make Christmas cards last year. (*Back to* JOEY:) Go on. Show the Chief the card.

JOEY *fishes through his wallet, finds a dog-eared photostat, hands it to* THE INDIAN, *who accepts curiously.*

INDIAN: Yeh k-yah hai? [What is this?]
MURPH: I made that with my own two cheeks. Tell him, Joe.
JOEY: Stupid, he don't speak English.
MURPH: It don't matter. He's interested, ain't he?
JOEY: You're a fink-jerk.
MURPH: Oooo. I'll give you noogies up the kazzooo. (*Takes the card away from* THE INDIAN *and explains.*) This is a Christmas card. I made it! I made it! Get me? Pussyface got us Christmas jobs last year. She got me one with the city. With the war on poverty. I ran the Xerox machine.
JOEY: Jesus. You really are stupid. He don't understand one word you're saying.
MURPH (*mimes the entire scene, slowly*): He's interested, ain't he? That's more than I can say for most of them. (*To* THE INDIAN:) Want to know how you can make your own Christmas cards with your simple Xerox 2400? It's easy. Watch. (*He mimes.*) First you lock the door to the stat room, so no one can bust in. Then you turn the machine on. Then you set the dial at the number of people you want to send cards to. Thirty, forty.
JOEY: Three or four.
MURPH: Right, fella. Then you take off your pants. And your underpants that's underneath. You sit on the glass. You push the little button. The lights flash. When the picture's developed, you write "Noel" across it! (*Pauses.*) That's how you make Christmas cards. (*Waits for a reaction from* THE INDIAN, *then turns back to* JOEY, *dismayed.*) He's waiting for the bus.
JOEY: Me too. Jesus. Am I ever late!
MURPH: Tell her to stuff it. You're a big boy now.
JOEY: She gets frightened, that's all. She really don't care how late I come in, as long as I tell her when I'm com-

ing. If I tell her one, and I don't get in until one-thirty, she's purple when I finally get in. (*Pauses.*) She's all right. Where's the Goddamned bus, huh? (*Calls across the park.*) Pussyface, did you steal the bus, you dirty old whore? Pussyface, I'm calling you! (*Pauses.*) She's all right, Murph. Christ, she's my mother. I didn't ask for her. She's all right.

MURPH: Who's all right? That Turkie-humper? (*To* THE INDIAN:) His old lady humps Turkies, you know that? (*Smiles, but* THE INDIAN *doesn't respond.*) Hey, Turkie's blowin' his cool a little. Least you got somebody waitin'. My old lady wouldn't know if I was gone a year.

JOEY: What? That Turkie-humper?

MURPH (*to* THE INDIAN): Hey! (THE INDIAN *jumps, startled.* MURPH *laughs.*) You got any little Indians runnin' around your teepee? No? Yeah? No? Aw, ya' stupid Indian. Where is the Goddamn bus?

JOEY: Let's walk it.

MURPH: Screw that. A hundred blocks? Besides, we gotta keep this old Turkie company, right? We couldn't let him stand all alone in this big ole city. Some nasty boys might come along and chew him up, right?

JOEY: We can walk it. Let the Indian starve.

MURPH: So walk it, jerk. I'm waiting with the Chief. (MURPH *stands next to* THE INDIAN.)

JOEY: Come on, we'll grab the subway.

MURPH: Joe, the trains are running crazy now. Anyway, I'm waitin' with my friend the Chief, here. You wanna go, go. (*Murmurs.*) Where is it, Chief? Is that it? Here it comes, huh?

JOEY (*considers it*): Yeah, we gotta watch out for Turkie. (JOEY *stands on the other side of* THE INDIAN, *who finally walks slowly back to the bus stop area.*)

MURPH: See that, Turkie, little Joe's gonna keep us company. That's nice, huh? (THE INDIAN *looks for the bus.*) You know, Joey, this Turk's a pain in my ass. He don't look at me when I talk to him.

JOEY: He oughta look at you when you talk. He oughta be polite.

They pass the card in a game. THE INDIAN *smiles.*

MURPH: I don't think he learned many smarts in Indiana. Any slob knows enough to look when they're being talked to. Huh?

JOEY: This ain't just any slob. This is a definite Turkie-Indian slob.

They pass the card behind their backs.

MURPH: He's one of them commie slobs, probably. War-mongering bastard. (*Flatly.*) Pinko here rapes all the little kids.

JOEY: Terrible thing. Too bad we can't give him some smarts. Maybe he could use a couple.

The game ends. JOEY *has the card as in a magic act.*

MURPH: We'll give him plenty of smarts. (*Calling him up-stage.*) Want some smarts? Chief?

INDIAN: Bna-ee mai toom-maree bah-at nah-hee sah-maj-sak-tah. Bus yah-han kis sa-may a-tee haj. K-yah mai sa-hee BUS STOP par shoon! [I can't understand you. Please? When is the bus due here? Am I at the right station?]

JOEY: Hey, look. He's talking out of the side of his mouth. Sure, that's right . . . Hey, Murph. Ain't Indian broads s'posed to have sideways breezers? Sure.

MURPH (*grins*): You mean chinks, Joey.

JOEY: Naw. Indian broads too. All them foreign broads. Their breezers are sideways. That's why them foreign cars have the back seat facing the side, right?

MURPH: Is that right, Turkie? Your broads have horizontal snatches?

INDIAN (*stares at him nervously*): Mai toom-haree bah-at nah-hee sah-maj sak-tah. [I can't understand you.]

MURPH (*repeating him in the same language*) : Toom-haree bah-at-nah-hee sah-maj sak-tah.

INDIAN (*recognizing the language finally. He speaks with incredible speed*) : Toom-haree bah-sha nah-hee sah-maj-tah. Moo-jhay mah-af kar-nah par ah-bhee moo-jhay toom-ha-ray desh aye kuh-chah hee din toh Hu-yay hain. Moo-jhay toom-ha-ree bah-sha see-kh-nay kah ah-bhee sah-mai hee nah-hee milah. Mai ahp-nay lar-kay say bih-chur gah-ya hoon. Oos-say toh toom-ha-ray desh may rah-tay chai sah-al hoh gah-ye hain. Jah-b doh mah-hee-nay pah-lay oos-kee mah kah inth-kahl moo-ah toh oos-nay moo-jhay ya-han booh-lah bheh-jha or mai ah gah-hay. Woh bah-ra hon-har lar-ka hai. Moo-jhay mah-af kar-nah kee majh-nay ah-bhee toom-ha-ree bah-sha na-hee see-knee par mai see-kh loon-gha. [Yes, that's correct. I can't understand your language. I'm sorry, but I've only been in your country for a few days. I haven't had time to understand your language. Please forgive me. I'm separated from my son. He's been living in your country for six years. When his mother died two months ago, he sent for me. I came immediately. He's a good son to his father. I'm sorry I haven't learned your language yet, but I shall learn.]

MURPH (*does a take. Flatly*) : This Turkie's a real pain in the ass.

JOEY: Naw. I think he's pretty interesting. I never saw an Indian before.

MURPH: Oh. It's fascinating. It's marvelous. This city's a regular melting pot. Turkies. Kikes like you. (*Pause.*) I even had me a real French lady once. (*Looks at the ground. Pauses.*) I thought I saw a dime here. (*Ponders.*) I knew it. (*He picks up a dime and pockets it proudly.*)

JOEY: A French lady, huh?

MURPH: Yep. A real French broad.

JOEY (*holds a beat*) : You been at your mother again?

MURPH (*hits him on the arm*) : Wise-ass. Just what nobody likes. A wise-ass.

JOEY : Where'd you have this French lady, huh?

MURPH : I found her in the park over there. (*Points.*) Just sitting on a bench. She was great. (*Boasts.*) A real *talent.*

JOEY : Yeah, sure thing. (*Calls into the park.*) Hello, talent. Hello, talent! (*Pauses.*) I had a French girl, too. (*Turns to avoid Murph's eyes, caught in a lie.*) Where the hell's that bus?

MURPH (*simply*) : Sure you did. Like the time you had a mermaid?

JOEY : You better believe I did. She wasn't really French. She just lived there a long time. I went to first grade with her. Geraldine. She was my first girl friend. (*Talks very quickly.*) Her old man was in the Army or something, 'cause they moved to France. She came back when we were in high school.

MURPH : Then what happened?

JOEY : Nothin'. She just came back, that's all.

MURPH : I thought you said you *had* her . . .

JOEY : No, she was just my girl friend.

MURPH : In high school?

JOEY : No, ya stoop. In the first grade. I just told you.

MURPH : You had her in the first grade?

JOEY : Jesus, you're stupid. She was my girl friend. That's all.

MURPH (*feigns excitement*) : Hey . . . that's a *sweet little story.* (*Flatly.*) What the hell's wrong with you?

JOEY : What do ya mean?

MURPH : First you say you had a French girl, then you say you had a girl friend in first grade, who went to France. What the hell kind of story's that?

JOEY : It's a true one, that's all. Yours is full of crap.

MURPH : What's full of crap?

JOEY : About the French lady in the park. You never had any French lady, unless you been at your own old lady again. Or maybe you've been at Pussyface?

MURPH: Jesus, you're lookin' for it, aren't you?

They pretend to fistfight.

JOEY: I mean, if you gotta tell lies to your best buddy, you're in bad shape, that's all.
MURPH (*gives* JOEY *a "high-sign"*): Best buddy? You?

They sign to THE INDIAN. *He returns the obscene gesture, thinking it a berserk American sign of welcome.*

JOEY: Is that how it is in Ceylon, sir?
MURPH: Say-lon? What the hell is say-long?
JOEY: See, ya jerk, Ceylon's part of India. That's where they grow tea.
MURPH: No kiddin'? Boy it's terrific what you can learn just standin' here with a schmuck like you. Tea, huh? (*To* THE INDIAN *he screams.*) Hey! (THE INDIAN *turns around, startled.*) How's your teabags? (*No response.*) No? (*To* JOEY.) Guess you're wrong again. He don't know teabags.
JOEY: Look at the bags under his eyes. That ain't chopped liver.

This is the transition scene: MURPH *screams* "Hey!"—THE INDIAN *smiles. They dance a war dance around him, beating a rhythm on the trashcans, hissing and cat-calling for a full minute.* MURPH *ends the dance with a final "Hey!"* THE INDIAN *jumps in fear. Now that they sense his fear, the comedy has ended.*

MURPH: Turkie looks like he's getting bored.
JOEY: Poor old Indian. Maybe he wants to play a game.
MURPH: You know any poor old Indian games?
JOEY: We could burn him at the stake. (*He laughs.*) That ain't such a terrible idea, you know. Maybe make an Indian stew.
MURPH: Naw, we couldn't burn a nice fellow like Turkie. That's nasty.
JOEY: We got to play a game. Pussyface always tells us to

play games. (*To the apartment, the back of the audience.*) Ain't that right, Pussyface? You always want us to play games.

MURPH: I know a game ...

JOEY: Yeah?

MURPH: Yeah. (*Screams at* THE INDIAN.) "Indian, Indian, Where's the Indian?"

JOEY: That's a sweet game. I haven't played that for years.

MURPH: Wise-ass. You want to play a game, don't you?

JOEY: Indian-Indian. Where's the Indian?

MURPH: Sure. It's just like ring-a-leave-eo. Only with a spin.

JOEY: That sounds terrific.

MURPH: Look. I spin the hell out of you until you're dizzy. Then you run across the street and get Pussyface. I'll grab the Indian and hide him. Then Pussyface and you come over here and try to find us.

JOEY: We're going to spin, huh?

MURPH: Sure.

JOEY: Who's going to clean up after you? Remember the Ferris wheel, big shot? All those happy faces staring up at you?

MURPH: I ain't the spinner. You're the spinner. I'll hide the Chief. Go on. Spin.

JOEY: How about if we set the rules as we go along? (*To* THE INDIAN.) How does that grab you, Chief?

INDIAN: Moo-jhay mah-af kar-nah. Mai toom-nakee bah-sha na-hee sah-maj sak-ta. [I'm sorry, but I can't understand your language.]

MURPH: He's talking Indiana again. He don't understand. Go on. Spin. I'll grab the Chief while you're spinning ... count the ten ... hide the Chief, while you're after Pussyface. Go on. Spin.

JOEY: I ain't going to spin. I get sick.

MURPH: Ain't you going to play?

JOEY: I'll play. But I can't spin any better than you can. I get sick. You know that. How about if you spin and I hide the Chief? You can get Pussyface. She likes you better than me, anyhow.

MURPH: Pussyface ain't home. You know that. She's in New Jersey.

JOEY: Then what the hell's the point of this game, anyway?

MURPH: It's just a game. We can pretend.

JOEY: You can play marbles for all I care. I just ain't going to spin, that's all. And neither are you. So let's forget the whole game.

MURPH (*fiercely*): Spin! Spin!

JOEY: You spin.

MURPH: Hey. I told you to spin.

MURPH *squares off against* JOEY *and slaps him menacingly.* JOEY *looks* MURPH *straight in the eye for a moment.*

JOEY: Okay. Big deal. So I'll spin. Then I get Pussyface, right? You ready to get the Chief?

MURPH: Will you stop talking and start spinning?

JOEY: All right. All right. Here I go. (JOEY *spins himself meekly, as* MURPH *goes toward* THE INDIAN *and the trash can.* JOEY *giggles as he spins ever so slowly.* MURPH *glances at* JOEY *as* JOEY *pretends.* MURPH *is confused.*) There. I spun. Is that okay?

MURPH: That's a spin?

JOEY: Well, it wasn't a fox trot.

MURPH: I told you to spin! Any slob knows that ain't no spin! Now spin, God damn it! Spin!

JOEY: This is stupid. You want to play games. You want a decent spin. You spin.

He walks straight to MURPH*—a challenge.* JOEY *slaps* MURPH. *He winces.*

MURPH (*squares off viciously. Raises his arms. Looks at* JOEY *cruelly. Orders*): Spin me.

JOEY *brings Murph's arms behind Murph's back and holds Murph's wrists firmly so that he is helpless.* JOEY *spins him. Slowly at first. Then faster. Faster. Joey's hostility is released; he laughs.*

JOEY: You wanted to spin. Spin. Spin.

JOEY *spins* MURPH *frantically.* THE INDIAN *watches in total horror, not knowing what to do; he cuddles next to the bus stop sign, his island of safety.*

MURPH (*screaming*): Enough, you little bastard.

JOEY (*continues to spin him*): Now *you* get Pussyface. Go on. (*Spins* MURPH *all the faster as in a grotesque dance gone berserk.*) I'll hide the Chief. This is your game! This is your game. *You* get Pussyface. I'll hide the Chief. Go on, Murphy. You want some more spin? (JOEY *has stopped the spinning now, as* MURPH *is obviously ill.*) You want to spin some more?

MURPH: Stop it, Joey. I'm sick.

JOEY (*spins* MURPH *once more around*): You want to spin some more, or are you going to get Pussyface and come find the Chief and me?

MURPH: You little bastard.

JOEY (*spins* MURPH *once again, still holding* MURPH *helpless with his arms behind his back*): I'll hide the Chief. YOU get Pussyface and find us. Okay? Okay? Okay?

MURPH: Okay . . . you bastard . . . okay.

JOEY: Here's one more for good luck.

JOEY *spins* MURPH *three more times, fiercely, then shoves him offstage.* MURPH *can be heard retching, about to vomit, during the final spins.* JOEY *then grabs* THE INDIAN, *who pulls back in terror.*

INDIAN: Na-hee bha-yee toom ah-b k-yah kah-rogay? [No, please, what are you going to do?]

JOEY: Easy, Chief. It's just a game. Murph spun out on us. It's just a game. I've got to hide you now.

Murph's final puking sounds can be heard well in the distance.

INDIAN: Na-hee na-hee bha-yee. Mai mah-afee mah-ng-ta. Hoon. [No. No. Please. I beg you.]

JOEY: Easy, Chief. Look. I promise you, this ain't for real. This is only a game. A game. Get it? It's all a game! Now I got to count to ten. (*Grabs* THE INDIAN *and forces him down behind a city litter basket. He covers The Indian's scream with his hand, as he slaps* THE INDIAN—*a horrifying sound.*) One. Two. Three. Murphy? (*He laughs.*) Four. Five. Murph? Come get us. Six. Seven. Pussyface is waiting. Eight. Nine. (*Pauses.*) Murphy? Murph? Hey, buddy. (*Stands up. Speaks.*) Ten. (*Lights are narrowing on* JOEY *and* THE INDIAN. THE INDIAN *tries to escape.* JOEY *subdues him easily.* JOEY *turns slowly back to* THE INDIAN, *who responds with open fear.*) Get up. Up. (*No response.*) Get up, Turkie. (*Moves to* THE INDIAN, *who recoils sharply.* JOEY *persists and pulls* THE INDIAN *to his feet.* THE INDIAN *shudders, stands and faces his captor.* THE INDIAN *shakes from fear and from a chill. There is a moment's silence as* JOEY *watches. He removes his own sweater and offers it to* THE INDIAN.) Here. Here. Put it on. It's okay. (THE INDIAN *is bewildered, but* JOEY *forces the sweater into his hands.*) Put it on. (THE INDIAN *stares at the sweater.* JOEY *takes it from his hands and begins to cover* THE INDIAN, *who is amazed.*) I hope I didn't hurt you too much. You okay? (*No response.*) You ain't sick too bad, huh? (*Pause.*) Huh? (*Checks* THE INDIAN *for cuts.*) You look okay. You're okay, huh? (*No response.*) I didn't mean to rough you up like that, but . . . you know. Huh? (THE INDIAN *raises his eyes to meet Joey's.* JOEY *looks down to avoid the stare.*) I hope you ain't mad at me or nothin'. (*Pause.*) Boy it's gettin' chilly. I mean, it's cold, right? Sure is quiet all of a sudden. Kind of spooky, huh? (*Calls.*) Hey, Murphy! (*Laughs aloud.*) Murph ain't a bad guy. He's my best buddy, see? I mean, he gets kinda crazy sometimes, but that's all. Everybody gets kind of crazy sometime, right?

(*No response.*) Jesus, you're a stupid Indian. Can't you speak any English? No? Why the hell did you come here, anyway? Especially if you can't talk any English. You ought to say something. Can't you even say "Thank you"?

THE INDIAN *recognizes those words, finally, and mimics them slowly and painfully.*

INDIAN (*in English, very British and clipped*): Thank you.

JOEY: I'll be Goddamned! You're welcome. (*Slowly, indicating for* THE INDIAN *to follow.*) You're welcome. (*He waits.*)

INDIAN (*in English*): You are welcome.

JOEY: That's terrific. You are welcome. (*Smiles, as though all is forgiven. In relief.*) How are you?

INDIAN: You are welcome.

JOEY: No. How are ya? (JOEY *is excited.* THE INDIAN *might be a second friend.*)

INDIAN (*in English—very "Joey"*): How are ya?

JOEY (*joyously*): Jesus. You'll be talking like us in no time! You're okay, huh? You ain't bleeding or anything. I didn't wanna hurt you none. But Murph gets all worked up. You know what I mean. He gets all excited. This ain't the first time, you know. No, sir!

INDIAN (*in English*): No, sir.

JOEY: That's right. He's especially crazy around broads.

INDIAN (*in English*): Broads.

JOEY (*forgetting that* THE INDIAN *is only mimicking*): That's right. Broads. (*Pauses and remembers, deeply.*) What am I yakking for? Tell me about India, huh? I'd like to go to India sometime. Maybe I will. You think I'd like India? India? (*No response.* THE INDIAN *recognizes the word, but doesn't understand the question.*) That's where you're from, ain't it? Jesus, what a stupid Indian. India! (*Spells the word.*) I-N-D-I-A. Nothin'. Schmuck. *India!*

INDIAN (*a stab in the dark*): Hindi?

JOEY: Yeah! Tell me about India! (*Long pause as they stand staring at each other.*) No? You're not talking, huh? Well, what do you want to do? Murph oughta be back soon. (*Discovers a coin in his pocket.*) You wanna flip for quarters? Flip? No? Look, a Kennedy half! (*Goes through three magic tricks with the coin:* [1] *He palms the coin, offers the obvious choice of hand, then uncovers the coin in his other hand.* THE INDIAN *raises his hand to his turban in astonishment.*) Like that, huh? ([2] *Coin is slapped on his breast.*) This hand right? Is it this hand, this hand? No, it's *this* hand! Back to your dumb act? Here. Here's the one you liked! (*Does* [1]. *This time* THE INDIAN *points to the correct hand instantly.*) You're probably some kind of hustler. Okay. Double or nothing. (*Flips.*) Heads, you live. Tails, you die. Okay? (*Uncovers the coin.*) I'll be a son of a bitch. You got Indian luck. Here. (*He hands the coin to* THE INDIAN.)

INDIAN (*stares in question*): Na-hff? [No?]

JOEY (*considers cheating*): Take it. You won. No, go ahead. Keep it. I ain't no Indian giver. (*Pause. He laughs at his own joke. No response.*) You ain't got no sense of humor, that's what. (*Stares upstage.*) Murph's my best buddy, you know? Me and him were buddies when we were kids. Me and Murph, all the time. And Maggie. His kid sister. (*Pause.*) I had Maggie once. Sort of. Well, kind of. Yeah, I had her. That's right. Murph don't know. Makes no difference now. She's dead, Maggie. (*Sings.*) "The worms crawl in, the worms crawl out." (*Speaks.*) What the hell difference does it make? *Right?*

INDIAN (*in English*): No, sir.

JOEY (*without noticing*): That's why Murph is crazy. That's why he gets crazy, I mean. She died seventeen, that's all. Seventeen. Just like *that*. Appendix. No one around. There was no one around. His old lady? Forget it! The old man took off years ago. All there was really was just Murph and Maggie. That's why he could take it. At home. You think my old lady's bad? She's nothing. His old lady's a pro. You know? She don't even make a living at it, either. That's the bitch of it. Not even a living. She's a dog. I mean, *I* wouldn't even pay her a nickel. Not a nickel. Not that I'd screw around with Murphy's old lady. Oh! Not that she doesn't try. She tries. Plenty. (*His fantasy begins.*) That's why I don't come around to his house much. She tries it all the time. She wouldn't charge me anything, probably. But it ain't right screwing your best buddy's old lady, right? I'd feel terrible if I did. She ain't that bad, but it just ain't right. I'd bet she'd even take Murph on. She probably tries it with him, too. That's the bitch of it. She can't even make a living. His own Goddamned mother. The other one—Pussyface. You think Pussyface is a help? That's the biggest joke yet. (THE INDIAN *is by now thoroughly confused on all counts. He recognizes the name "Pussyface," and reacts slightly. Seeing Joey's anxiety, he cuddles him. For a brief moment they embrace—an insane father-and-son tableau. Note: Be careful here.*) Pussyface. There's a brain. You see what she gave us for Christmas? (*Fishes his knife out of his pocket.*) Knives. Brilliant, huh? Murph's up on a rap for slicing a kid, and she gives us knives for Christmas. To whittle with. She's crazier than Murphy. Hah. (*Flashes his open knife at* THE INDIAN, *who misinterprets the move as spelling disaster.* THE INDIAN *waits, carefully scrutinizing* JOEY, *until* JOEY *begins to look away.* JOEY *now wanders to the spot where he pushed* MURPH *offstage.*) Hey, Murph! (THE INDIAN *moves slowly to the other side of the stage.* JOEY *sees his move at once and races after him, thinking* THE INDIAN *was running away.*) Hey. Where are you going? (THE INDIAN *knows he'll be hit. He tries to explain with mute gestures and attitude. It's futile. He knows at once and hits* JOEY *as best he can and races across the stage.* JOEY *recovers from the blow and starts after him, as* THE INDIAN *murmurs one continuous fright-*

ening scream. JOEY *dives after* THE INDIAN *and tackles him on the other side of the stage.* THE INDIAN *fights more strongly than ever, but Joey's trance carries him ferociously into this fight. He batters* THE INDIAN *with punches to the body.* THE INDIAN *squeals as* JOEY *sobs.*) You were gonna run off. Right? Son of a bitch. You were gonna tell Murphy.

THE INDIAN *makes one last effort to escape and runs the length of the stage, screaming a bloodcurdling, anguished scream.* MURPH *enters, stops, stares incredulously as* THE INDIAN *runs into his open arms.* JOEY *races to* THE INDIAN *and strikes a karate chop to the back of his neck.* JOEY *is audibly sobbing.* THE INDIAN *drops to the stage as a bull in the ring, feeling the final thrust of the sword . . .* JOEY *stands frozen above him.* MURPH *stares, first at* JOEY *and then at* THE INDIAN.

MURPH: Pussyface isn't home yet. She's still in New Jersey. Ring-a-leave-eo.

JOEY (*sobbing, senses his error*): Indians are dumb.

MURPH (*stares again at* JOEY. *Then to* THE INDIAN. *Spots Joey's sweater on* THE INDIAN. *Fondles it, then stares at* JOEY *viciously*): Pussyface isn't home. I rang her bell. She don't answer. I guess she's still on vacation. She ruined our game.

JOEY (*sobbing*): Oh, jumping Jesus Christ. Jesus. Jesus. Jesus. Indians are dumb.

MURPH: Pussyface ruins everything. She don't really care about our games. She ruins our games. Just like Indians. They don't know how to play our games either.

JOEY: Indians are dumb. Dumb.

He sobs. MURPH *slaps* JOEY *across the face. He straightens up and comes back to reality.*

MURPH: What the hell's going on?

JOEY: He tried to run. I hit him.

MURPH: Yeah. I saw that. You hit him, all right. (*Stares at* THE INDIAN.) Is he alive?

THE INDIAN *groans, pulls himself to his knees.*

JOEY: He was fighting. I hit him.
MURPH: Okay, you hit him.

THE INDIAN *groans again. Then he speaks in a plea.*

INDIAN (*praying*): Moo-jhay or nah sah-tao. Maih-nay toom-hara k-yah bigarah hai. Moo-jhay or nah sah-tao. Moo-jhay in-seh. [Please. Don't hurt me any more. What have I done? Please don't hurt me. Don't let them hurt me.]
MURPH: He's begging for something. Maybe he's begging for his life. Maybe he is. Sure, maybe he is.
JOEY (*embarrassed, starts to help* THE INDIAN *to his feet*): C'mon there, Chief. Get up and face the world. C'mon, Chief. Everything's going to be all right.
MURPH: What's got into you, anyway?
JOEY: C'mon, Chief. Up at the world. Everything's okay.

THE INDIAN *ad libs words of pleading and pain.*

MURPH: Leave him be. (*But* JOEY *continues to help* THE INDIAN.) Leave him be. What's with you? Hey, Joey! I said leave him be! (MURPH *pushes* JOEY *and* THE INDIAN *pulls back with fear.*)
JOEY: Okay, Murph. Enough's enough.
MURPH: Just tell me what the hell's wrong with you?
JOEY: He tried to run away, that's all. Change the subject. Change the subject. It ain't important. I hit him, that's all.
MURPH: Okay, so you hit him.
JOEY: Okay! Where were you? Sick. Were you a little bit sick? I mean, you couldn't have been visiting, 'cause there ain't no one to visit, right?
MURPH: What *do* you mean?

JOEY: Where the hell were you? (*Looks at* MURPH *and giggles.*) You're a little green there, Irish.

MURPH: You're pretty funny. What the hell's so funny?

JOEY: Nothing's funny. The Chief and I were just having a little pow-wow and we got to wondering where you ran off to. Just natural for us to wonder, ain't it? (*To* THE INDIAN.) Right, Chief.

MURPH: Hey, look at that. Turkie's got a woolly sweater just like yours. Ain't that a terrific coincidence? You two been playing strip poker?

JOEY: Oh, sure. Strip poker. The Chief won my sweater and I won three of his feathers and a broken arrow. (*To* THE INDIAN, *he feigns a deep authoritative voice.*) You wonder who I am, don't you? Perhaps this silver bullet will help to identify me? (*Extends his hand.* THE INDIAN *peers into Joey's empty palm quizzically. As he does,* MURPH *quickly taps the underside of Joey's hand, forcing the hand to rise and slap The Indian's chin sharply.* THE INDIAN *pulls back at the slap.* JOEY *turns on* MURPH, *quickly.*) What the hell did you do that for, ya' jerk. The Chief didn't do nothing.

MURPH: Jesus, you and your Chief are pretty buddy-buddy, ain't you? (*Mimics* JOEY.) "The Chief didn't do nothing." Jesus. You give him your sweater. Maybe you'd like to have him up for a beer . . .

JOEY: Drop it, Murph. You're giving me a pain in the ass.

MURPH (*retorts fiercely*): You little pisser. Who the hell do you think you're talking to?

The telephone rings in the booth. They are all startled, especially THE INDIAN, *who senses hope.*

JOEY (*after a long wait, speaking the obvious flatly*): It's the phone.

MURPH (*to* THE INDIAN): The kid's a whiz. He guessed that right away.

The phone rings a second time.

JOEY: Should we answer it?
MURPH: What for? Who'd be calling here? It's a wrong number.

The phone rings menacingly a third time. Suddenly THE INDIAN *darts into the phone booth and grabs the receiver.* JOEY *and* MURPH *are too startled to stop him until he has blurted out his hopeless plea, in his own language.*

INDIAN: Prem k-yah woh may-rah ar-kah hai. Prem (pray-em) bay-tah moo-jhay bachah-low. Mai fah ns ga-yah hoon yeh doh goon-day moo-jhay mar ra-hay hain. Mai ba-hoot ghah-bara gaya hoon. Pray-em. [Prem? Is this my son? Prem? Please help me. I'm frightened. Please help me. Two boys are hurting me . . . I'm frightened. Please. Prem?]

THE INDIAN *stops talking sharply and listens. He crumbles as the voice drones the wrong reply. He drops the receiver and stares with horror at the boys.* MURPH *realizes The Indian's horror and begins to laugh hysterically.* JOEY *stares silently.* THE INDIAN *begins to mumble and weep. He walks from the phone booth. The voice is heard as a drone from the receiver. The action freezes.*

MURPH (*laughing*): What's the matter, Turkie? Don't you have a dime? Give Turkie a dime, Joe. Give him a dime.
JOEY: Jesus Christ. I'd hate to be an Indian.
MURPH: Hey, the paper! C'mon, Joey, get the paper from him. We'll call the Bronx.
JOEY: Cut it out, Murph. Enough's enough.
MURPH: Get the frigging piece of paper. What's the matter with you, anyway?
JOEY: I just don't think it's such a terrific idea, that's all.
MURPH: You're chicken. That's what you are.
JOEY: Suppose his son has called the police. What do you think? You think he hasn't called the police? He knows the old man don't speak any English. He called the police. Right? And they'll trace our call.

MURPH: You're nuts. They can't trace any phone calls. Anyway, we'll be gone from here. You're nuts.

JOEY: I don't want to do it.

MURPH: For Christ's sake. They can't trace nothing to nobody. Who's going to trace? Get the paper.

JOEY: Get it yourself. Go on. Get it yourself. I ain't going to get it.

MURPH: C'mon, Joey. It's not real. This is just a game. It ain't going to hurt anybody. You know that. It's just a game.

JOEY: Why don't we call somebody else? We'll call somebody else and have the Indian talk. That makes sense. Imagine if an Indian called you up and talked to you in Indian. I bet the Chief would go for that all right. Jesus, Murphy.

MURPH: Get the paper and picture.

INDIAN: Ah-b toom k-yah kah-rogay. Moo-jhay mah-af kar-doh bha-yee maih-nay soh-cha tah key woh may-rah bay-tah pray-em hai. Moo-jhay telephone kar raha. Mai-nay soh-chah thah sha-yahd woh. Pray-em hoh. [What are you going to do now? I'm sorry. I thought that was my son, Prem. I thought that it might be Prem calling me on the telephone. Prem. That's who I thought it was. Prem.]

MURPH: Prem. That's the name. (*Plays the rhyme.*)

INDIAN: Pray-aim. [Prem?]

MURPH: Yes, Prem. I want to call Prem. Give me the paper with his name.

INDIAN: Toom pray-aim kay ba-ray may k-yah kah ra-hay. Ho toom-nay pray-aim koh kyah key-yah. Toom oos-kay bah-ray may k-yah jan-tay ho k-yah toom jan-tay ho woh kah-han hai. [What are you saying about Prem? Prem is my son. What have you done to Prem? What do you know about him? Do you know where he is?]

MURPH: Shut up already and give me the paper.

JOEY: Jesus, Murph.

MURPH (*turning* THE INDIAN *around so that they face each*

other) : This is ridiculous. (*Searches* THE INDIAN, *who resists a bit at first, and then not at all. Finally,* MURPH *finds the slip of paper.*) I got it. I got it. Terrific. "Prem Gupta." In the Bronx. In the frigging Bronx. This is terrific. (*Pushes* THE INDIAN *to* JOEY.) Here. Hold him.

INDIAN : Toom k-yah kar ra-hay ho k-yah toom pray-aim k-oh boo-lah ra-hay ho. [What are you doing? Are you going to call my son?]

MURPH : Shut him up. (*Fishes for a dime.*) Give me a dime, God damn it. This is terrific.

JOEY (*finds the coins in his pocket*) : Here's two nickels. (*Hands them over.*) I think this is a rotten idea, that's what I think. (*Pauses.*) And don't forget to pay me back those two nickels either.

MURPH : Just shut up. (*Dials the information operator.*) Hello. Yeah, I want some information . . . I want a number up in the Bronx . . . Gupta . . . G-U-P-T-A . . . an Indian kid . . . His first name's Prem . . . P-R-E-M . . . No . . . I can't read the street right . . . Wait a minute. (*Reads the paper to himself.*) For Christ's sake. How many Indians are up in the Bronx? There must be only one Indian named Gupta.

JOEY : What's she saying?

MURPH : There are two Indians named Gupta. (*To the operator.*) Is the two of them named Prem? (*Pauses.*) Well, that's what I told you . . . Jesus . . . wait a minute . . . okay . . . okay. Say that again . . . Okay . . . Okay . . . Right. Okay . . . thanks. (*Hurries quickly to return the coins to the slot.* GUPTA *mumbles. To* JOEY.) Don't talk to me. (*Dials.*) Six . . . seven-four. Oh. One. Seven, seven. (*Pauses.*) It's ringing. It's ringing. (*Pauses.*) Hello. (*Covers the phone with his hand.*) I got him! Hello? Is this Prem Gupta? Oh swell. How are you? (*To* JOEY.) I got the kid!

THE INDIAN *breaks from Joey's arm and runs to the telephone . . .* MURPH *sticks out his leg and holds* THE

INDIAN *off.* THE INDIAN *fights, but seems weaker than ever.*

INDIAN (*screams*): Cree-payah moo-jhay ad-nay lar-kay say bah-at kar-nay doh. [Please let me talk to my son.] (MURPH *slams* THE INDIAN *aside violently.* JOEY *stands frozen, watching.* THE INDIAN *wails and finally talks calmly, as in a trance.*) Cree-payah moo-jhay ahd-nay lar-kay say bah-at kar-nay doh. Mai toom-haray hah-th jor-tah hoom mai toom-hay joh mango-gay doon-gar bus moo-jhay oos-say bah-at kar-nay doh. [Please let me talk to my son. Oh, Prem. Please, I beg of you. Please. I'll give you anything at all. Just tell me what you want of me. Just let me talk with my son. Won't you, please?]

MURPH *glares at* THE INDIAN, *who no longer tries to interfere, as it becomes obvious that he must listen to even the language he cannot understand.*

MURPH: Just listen to me, will you, Gupta? I don't know where the hell your old man is, that's why I'm calling. We found an old elephant down here in Miami and we thought it must be yours. You can't tell for sure whose elephant is whose. You know what I mean? (MURPH *is laughing now.*) What was that? Say that again. I can't hear you too well. All the distance between us, you know what I mean? It's a long way down here, you follow me? No. I ain't got no Indian. I just got an elephant. And he's eating all my peanuts. Gupta, you're talking too fast. Slow down.

INDIAN: Pray-aim bhai-yah moo-jhay ah-kay lay ja-oh moo-jhay ap-nay lar-kay say bah-at kar-nay doh moo-jhay oos-say bah-at k-yohn nah-hee kar-nay day-tay. [Prem! Prem! Please come and get me. Please let me talk to my son, mister. Why don't you let me talk to my son?]

JOEY *leaps on* THE INDIAN; *tackles him, lies on top of him in front of the telephone booth.*

MURPH: That was the waiter. I'm in an Indian restaurant. (*Pauses.*) Whoa. Slow down, man. That was nobody. That was just a myth. Your imagination. (*Pauses. Screams into the receiver.*) Shut up, damn you! And listen. Okay? Okay. Are you listening? (MURPH *tastes the moment. He silently clicks the receiver back to the hook. To* JOEY.) He was very upset. (*To* THE INDIAN.) He was very upset. (*Pauses.*) Well, what the hell's the matter with you? I only told him we found an elephant, that's all. I thought maybe he lost his elephant.

THE INDIAN *whimpers.*

INDIAN: Toom-nay ai-saw k-yohn ki-yah toom-nay may-ray lar-kay koh k-yah ka-hah hai. [Why have you done this? What have you said to my son?]

MURPH: You don't have to thank me, Turkie. I only told him your elephant was okay. He was probably worried sick about your elephant. (MURPH *laughs.*) This is terrific, Joey. Terrific. You should have hear the guy jabber. He was so excited he started talking in Indian just like the Chief. He said that Turkie here and him got separated today. Turkie's only been in the city one day. You're pretty stupid, Turkie. One day in the city . . . and look at the mess you've made. You're pretty stupid. He's stupid, right?

JOEY: Yeah. He's stupid.

MURPH: Hold him. We'll try again. Sure.

THE INDIAN *jumps on* MURPH. *He tries to strangle* MURPH.

MURPH (*screaming*): Get him off of me! (JOEY *pulls* THE INDIAN *down to the ground as* MURPH *pounds the booth four times, screaming hideous sounds of aggression. With this tension released he begins to call, fierce but controlled, too controlled.* MURPH *takes the dime from his pocket, shows it to* JOEY, *and recalls the number. Talking into receiver. He dials number again and waits for reply.*) Hello? Is this Gupta again? Oh, hello there . . . I'm calling back to complain about your elephant . . . hey, slow down, will you? Let me do the talking. Okay? Your elephant is a terrific pain in the balls to me, get it? Huh? Do you follow me so far? (*Pauses.*) I don't know what you're saying, man . . . how about if I do the talking, all right? . . . Your elephant scares hell out of me and my pal here. We don't like to see elephants on the street. Spiders and snakes are okay, but elephants scare us. Elephants . . . yeah, that's right. Don't you get it, pal? . . . Look, we always see spiders and snakes. But we never expect to see an elephant . . . What do you mean "I'm crazy"? I don't know nothing about your old man . . . I'm talking about your elephant. Your elephant offends the hell out of me. So why don't you be a nice Indian kid and come pick him up . . . that's right . . . wait a minute . . . I'll have to check the street sign. (*Covers the receiver.*) This is terrific. (*Talks again into the telephone.*) Jesus, I'm sorry about that. There don't seem to be no street sign . . . that's a bitch. I guess you lose your elephant . . . well, what do you expect me to do, bring your elephant all the way up to the Bronx? Come off it, pal. You wouldn't ever bring my elephant home. I ain't no kid, you know! I've lost a couple of elephants in my day. (*Listens.*) Jesus, you're boring me now . . . I don't know what the hell you're talking about. Maybe you want to talk to your elephant . . . huh? (*Turns to* THE INDIAN.) Here, come talk to your "papoose."

He offers the telephone. THE INDIAN *stares in disbelief, then grabs the telephone from Murph's hands and begins to chatter wildly.*

INDIAN: Pray-aim, bhai-yah Pray-aim moo-jhay ah-kay lay jah-oh k-yah? Moo-jhay nah-hee pa-tah mai kah-han hoo-n moo-jhay ah-hp-nay gha-ar lay chah-low ya-hahn do-ah bad-mash lar-kay. Jo bah-hoot kha-tar-nahk hai-don-say mai nah-hee bah-cha sak-tah ah-pa-nay koh toom aik-dam moo-jhay ah-kay. [Prem? Oh, Prem. Please come and take me away . . . what? I don't know where I am . . . Please come and take me to your house . . . please? There are two bad people. Two young men. They are dangerous. I cannot protect myself from them. Please . . . You must come and get me.]

MURPH *takes his knife from his pocket, cuts the line.* THE INDIAN *almost falls flat on his face as the line from the receiver to the phone box is cut, since he has been leaning away from* MURPH *and* JOEY *during his plea.*

MURPH: You've had enough, Chief. (MURPH *laughs aloud.*)

INDIAN (*not at once realizing the line must be connected, continues to talk into the telephone in Hindi*): Pray-aim, Pray-aim, ya-hahn aa-oh sah-rak kah nah-am hai—yeh toom-nay k-yah key-yah. [Prem. Prem. Please come here. The street sign reads . . .] (*He now realizes he has been cut off and stares dumbly at the severed cord as* MURPH *waves the severed cord in his face.*) Toom-nay yeh k-yoh key-yah? [What have you done?]

MURPH: There it is, Turkie. Who you talkin' to?

INDIAN (*to* JOEY, *screaming a father's fury and disgust*): Toom-nay yeh k-yohn key-yah cri-payah may-ree mah-dah-d kah-roho. [Why have you done this? Please. Please help me.]

JOEY *has been standing throughout the entire scene, frozen in terror and disgust. He walks slowly toward* MURPH, *who kicks* THE INDIAN. JOEY *bolts from the stage, muttering one continuous droning sob.*

MURPH (*screaming*): Go ahead, Joey. Love him. Love him like a mother. Hey? Joey? What the hell's the matter? C'mon, buddy? (*Turns to* THE INDIAN, *takes his knife and cuts The Indian's hand, so blood is on the knife.*) Sorry, Chief. This is for my buddy, Joey. And for Pussy-face. (*Calls offstage.*) Joey! Buddy! What the hell's the matter? (*Races from the stage after* JOEY.) Joey! Wait up. Joey! I killed the Indian!

He exits. THE INDIAN *stares dumbly at his hand, dripping blood. He then looks to the receiver and talks into it.*

INDIAN: Pray-aim, Pray-aim, mai ah-pa-nay lar-kay key ah-wah-az k-yon nah-hee soon sak-tah Pray-aim! Toom-nay may-ray sah-ahth aih-saw k-yohn key-yaw bay-tah Pray-aim, k-yah toom ho? [Prem. Prem.] (*He walks center stage, well away from the telephone booth.* [Why can I not hear my son, Prem? Why have you done this to me?] *Suddenly the telephone rings again. Once. Twice.* THE INDIAN *is startled. He talks into the receiver, while he holds the dead line in his bleeding hand.*) [Prem? Is that you? Prem?] (*The telephone rings a third time.*) Pray-aim, Pray-aim, bay-tah k-yah toom ho—[Prem. Prem? Is that you?] (*A fourth ring.* THE INDIAN *knows the telephone is dead.*) Pray-aim Pray-aim—moo-jhay bah-chald Pray-aim. [Prem. Prem. Help me. Prem.]

As the telephone rings a fifth time, in the silence of the night, the sounds of two boys' singing is heard.

FIRST BOY:
I walk the lonely streets at night,
A'lookin' for your door . . .

SECOND BOY:
I look and look and look and look . . .

FIRST BOY *and* SECOND BOY:
But, baby, you don't care.
But, baby, no one cares.
But, baby, no one cares.

Their song continues to build as they repeat the lyrics, so the effect is one of many, many voices. The telephone continues its unanswered ring. THE INDIAN *screams a final anguished scream of fury to the boys offstage. The telephone rings a final ring as* THE INDIAN *screams.*

INDIAN (*desperately, holding the telephone to the audience as an offer. He speaks in English into the telephone. The only words he remembers are those from his lesson*): How are you? You're welcome. You're welcome. Thank you. (*To the front.*) Thank you!

Blackout

Father Uxbridge Wants to Marry

Frank Gagliano

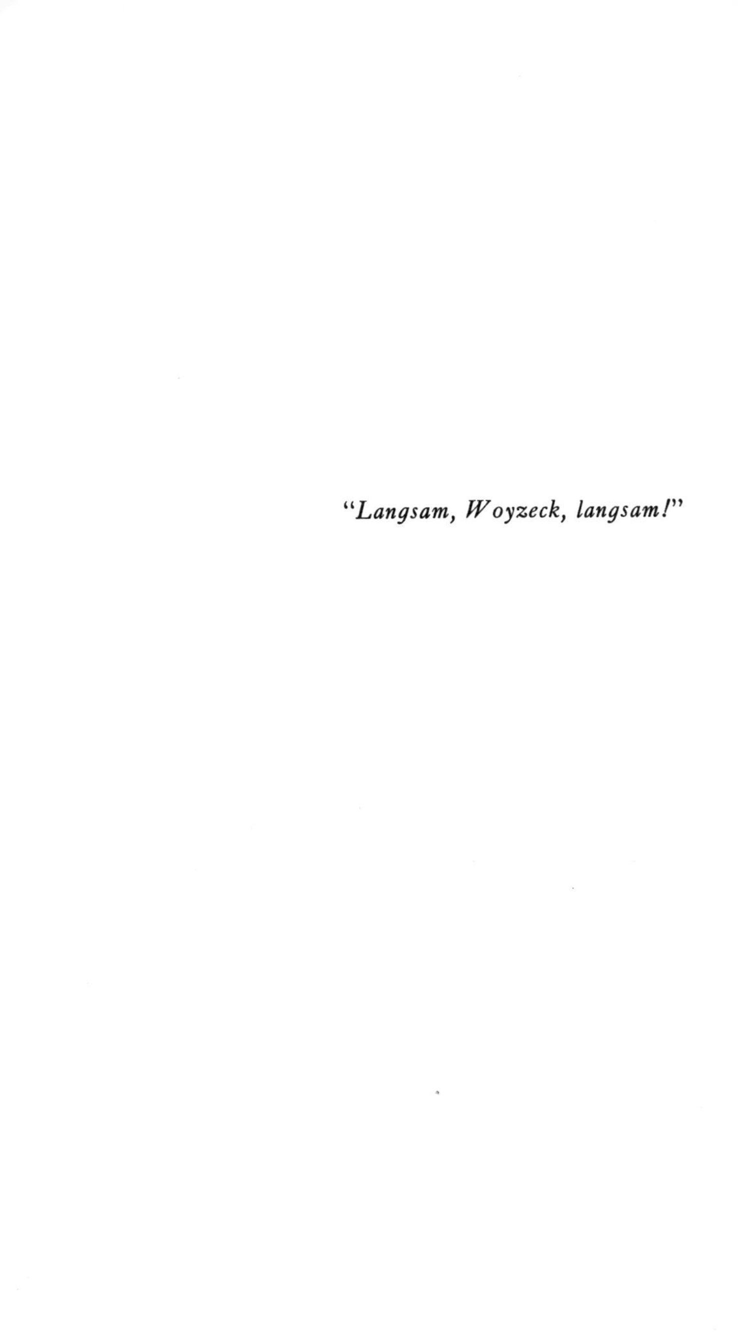

"Langsam, Woyzeck, langsam!"

FRANK GAGLIANO

Father Uxbridge Wants to Marry is a talented, difficult play which takes Gagliano into new dramatic terrain and away from the naturalism of his well-received *Night of the Dunce*. His play is conceived in that nether world which mixes moment and memory, speech and lingering sounds. The hero of Gagliano's tale is a beleaguered simpleton named Morden who struggles to get outside himself. He is not merely vulnerable, he is punished by experience. His head rings with Bach oratorios, and the fragmented frequencies of electronic music which deny the inherited sense of cosmic coherence. He has no skills; he has no keen intelligence. He is plagued with both guilt and hatred for a world which never stands still long enough for comprehension. He would kill Debden, the woman he loves, rather than lose her; he would destroy the priests of the Church to whom he comes for guidance, only to find they are becoming "modern." Conscious of sinning, yet continually betrayed by the world, he envisions himself at the Crucifixion, not as the Roman nailing Christ to the cross, but as the blunt pounding of hammer meeting nail.

When the play opens, Morden is running an elevator and being informed by the landlady that he is being replaced by an Otis Automatic. "There's an Otis in the Vatican" she tells him. The elevator stalls, the landlady, stuffing herself with candies, begins to choke. Morden's life flashes in front of him in this allegory of heaven and hell. He yearns for transcendence; "as if a great mouth was at the bottom of the shaft, and it was blowing this cage with such force that it took no effort at all to smash me right on through the roof . . ."

To this drooping knight of faith, his work, like his religious alternatives, do not have the thrill of free choice. Father Uxbridge reminds him "Either/Or. Push or manipulate, Morden." Morden cannot make Kierkegaard's leap, not, at least, in the twentieth century. Gagliano's vision of the clergy is hilarious and almost too strong for the play's intentions. Uxbridge, the old guard, explains his Billy Graham rhetoric this way:

> Things are changing. Did you know, Morden, that jazz has been allowed in the Mass? And a Catholic priest recently addressed the Masons? Why, if this keeps up, one of these days I may even have to address the Jesuits. (*Crosses himself.*)

Uxbridge goes on to confess "The murderous soul. That's my shtick."

Morden receives the buffets of the new, swinging priesthood from Father Ongar who replaces the fire and brimstone of Uxbridge. Ongar gives a hippie sermon that burlesques the attempts to decorate old, unfirm foundations with gaudy exteriors:

> My brethren. Michelangelo Buonarotti, that clever wop fairy, painted a vision of the last judgment in which some of humanity, surprised—but not too put out, for after all, *they* had it made—are allowing themselves to be hoisted up to a glorious heaven in the arms of muscular angels . . . We'll annihilate the past—for we've got to find our own way to His cruelty—by going on a psychedelic trip. I, leading the way, of course. And the whole church will be a Chagall world. I'll put red velvet on all the walls and everyone in their Sunday froufrou will float fapitzt in a blue-green haze.

Gagliano's ability to make language memorable (Morden speaks of his aged mother whining "like a car idling") is part of this craftsmanship. *Uxbridge* has a dark humor: the names of his characters are all taken from stops on the London underground—suggesting a subterranean world as well as a joke. Morden never goes through the roof. God—the Angel of Death—is as silent as the mute little girl called Angel whom Morden wants to adopt. Gagliano's vision is a complex one—even galling at times—but at every point in the play, we are conscious of a craftsman, testing his talent in a society which is not interested in long, hard looks at serious questions.

Father Uxbridge Wants to Marry was first performed at the American Place Theatre, in New York City, on October 12, 1967. It was directed by Melvin Bernhardt and designed by Douglas Schmidt, with lighting by John Gleason and special sound and music by James Reichert. The Bach arias were sung by Sandra Gagliano. The cast was as follows:

MORDEN	Eugene Roche
MRS. BETHNAL-GREEN THE MOTHER STEPNEY GREEN DEBDEN	Olympia Dukakis
FATHER UXBRIDGE	John Coe
FATHER ONGAR	Ken Kercheval
ANGEL	Carol Carpenter

Prior to the New York City production, the play was given a staged reading on July 29, 1967, at the Eugene O'Neill Memorial Theatre Foundation in Waterford, Connecticut, during the Summer Playwrights' Conference. The cast was as follows: Tom Adkins as Morden, Tresa Hughes as all the women, John Coe as Father Uxbridge, Charles Kimbrough as Father Ongar, and Rebecca Hughes as Angel. The author wishes to acknowledge their contribution to the play's growth.

CHARACTERS

(in order of appearance)

MRS. BETHNAL-GREEN

MORDEN

FATHER UXBRIDGE

ANGEL

THE MOTHER

STEPNEY GREEN

DEBDEN

FATHER ONGAR

THE SINGER

All the characters, except Morden and Angel, wear masks, as described in the text.

Mrs. Bethnal-Green, the Mother, Debden, and Stepney Green should be played by the same actress. However, if one actress with the total skills is not available, four different actresses can be used.

Morden's Mother may be a stuffed dummy propped up in a wheel chair, as in the New York production, or a live actress. In either case, the voice is on tape.

TIME: *The present*
PLACE: *An elevator, a Rectory, and various limbo areas*

I

THE SCENE: *An elevator, which can be placed downstage center and split in half when Morden's mind fragments, leaving a small permanent platform which Morden uses throughout. (This is what was done in the New York production.) The elevator, however, can be a permanent platform upstage right or, indeed, just a specially lighted area with a bench for Mrs. Bethnal-Green to sit on. Downstage right: another bench.*
BEFORE CURTAIN: *The whirring sound of an elevator, which continues in the background until indicated.*
AT CURTAIN: *Mrs. Bethnal-Green is seated on the bench in the elevator. Morden is standing at the old-fashioned hand-lever. Mrs. Bethnal-Green's mask has puffy red cheeks and a perpetual smirk. She is eating a jumbo candy bar. At her feet, a nylon-net shopping bag filled, mostly, with boxes of candy. Morden does not wear a mask.*

MRS. BETHNAL-GREEN: Well, Mr. Morden, and how do you like being replaced by an automatic elevator?

In the background, a choir of angels sings one chord.

MORDEN: What? What was that, Mrs. Bethnal-Green?
MRS. BETHNAL-GREEN: I said, how do you like being replaced by an automatic elevator?

The choir of angels sings one chord.

MORDEN: I don't understand, Mrs. Bethnal-Green.

MRS. BETHNAL-GREEN: Well, I'm not going to repeat myself again, Mr. Morden. If you can't grasp a simple . . . Mr. Morden, you did receive my letter?

MORDEN: Letter?

MRS. BETHNAL-GREEN: Stating that Mr. Whitechapel, Realtor for this and a host of other buildings of similar stature, has declared through me that you are to be let go.

MORDEN: Fired? I'm to be fired?

The choir of angels sings one chord.

MRS. BETHNAL-GREEN: Replaced.

The choir of angels sings one chord.

By an automatic elevator.

The choir of angels sings one chord.

MORDEN: No. I didn't receive any letter.

MRS. BETHNAL-GREEN: Oh, it's galling. It really is. You want so to do a right thing right. Well, I did send that letter special delivery. And registered. Forty-five cents extra, Mr. Morden! What a waste! And you know how I hate waste, Mr. Morden.

MORDEN: And you mean there's nothing to be done?

MRS. BETHNAL-GREEN: Nothing to be done.

MORDEN: What if I talked to Mr. Whitechapel?

MRS. BETHNAL-GREEN: You? Personally talk? That's a funny thought, Mr. Morden. Droll, even. Nobody talks to Mr. Whitechapel. Don't you understand? He sent a letter. Bona fide. Signed. Well, not signed by him, but by someone for him. No, Mr. Morden, it's over. You are being replaced by an automatic elevator. I hope you understand that. I hope you accept it deep down. Because it's irrevocable. Irreversible. Unalterable. Definite, Mr. Morden.

Pause.

MORDEN: Well, I've been replaced before, Mrs. Bethnal-Green. Never by something mechanical, though. But I guess I'll survive.

The choir of angels sings one chord.

MRS. BETHNAL-GREEN: You're a lucky man. I sometimes wonder if I shall. I just came from the doctor, Mr. Morden. "Don't do this." "Don't eat that." He even told me to give up sweets. (*She bites into a candy bar.*)

MORDEN: It's easier now since I don't have an invalid mother to support. (*Bitterly.*) Still, whenever I visit, the nurses expect a little something.

MRS. BETHNAL-GREEN: Yes, you healthy people have it all over us. I mean, what good is having money when you have to give up sweets? What's life all about if you have to give up what has most meaning for you? I mean, here I am Manager of this fine building and still . . .

MORDEN: Actually, I'm never in the tip-toppest of condition, Mrs. Bethnal-Green. There was a time when I had to sell my blood a lot. I think that tended to weaken me.

MRS. BETHNAL-GREEN: Sell your blood? Really, Mr. Morden, Mr. Whitechapel is giving you a month's severance pay! I hope you know that's above and beyond . . .

MORDEN: A month—a month goes by fast. But that is, indeed, a nice settlement, Mrs. Bethnal-Green.

MRS. BETHNAL-GREEN: Well, I should say. Why, we're one big family to Mr. Whitechapel. He said just that many times in those wonderful inter-house memos of his. No. He's not about to let one of his children go out without some financial cushion. So you see, we have tried to be fair. And I hardly expected you to be so morbid, Mr. Morden. I mean, I don't see why you feel you must talk about "selling blood"! A month is sufficient time to find another position.

MORDEN: Sometimes. But I'm getting on.

MORDEN'S VOICE (*off, echoing*): And where are you now, Father Uxbridge, with your jobs?

MORDEN: And when you reach a certain age nowadays, few firms, if any, will consider you.

MRS. BETHNAL-GREEN: Nonsense. A man who has something to offer will always be considered.

MORDEN: Well, I don't have much to offer, you see. But I'm still a religious man, and if it's God's will . . .

MRS. BETHNAL-GREEN (*amused*): You think it's God who wants an automatic elevator, Mr. Morden?

MORDEN: I'm sure a simple man like myself wouldn't know, Mrs. Bethnal-Green. But I'll try to get up the courage to ask Him when I finally smash through the roof.

The choir of angels sings one chord.

MRS. BETHNAL-GREEN: Smash through the—what—Mr. Morden?

MORDEN: Just my manner of speaking, Mrs. Bethnal-Green.

MRS. BETHNAL-GREEN: You mean dying, don't you. If you mean dying, say dying. On second thought, don't. I don't want to hear about dying.

Sound of elevator whirring stops. MORDEN *and* MRS. BETHNAL-GREEN *count to ten silently. Only their lips move. Whirring noise up. The elevator has started again.*

MRS. BETHNAL-GREEN: You really want to know who wants an automatic elevator, Mr. Morden? I'll tell you who wants an automatic elevator. *I* want an automatic elevator. And that's one of the reasons why; that stopping to the count of ten, I mean.

Sound of whirring noise out. The elevator has stopped again. MORDEN *and* MRS. BETHNAL-GREEN *silently count to ten. The elevator starts up.*

MRS. BETHNAL-GREEN: You see? You just can't have an elevator that stops and starts whenever it pleases. Not in this day and age, Mr. Morden. Oh, it's not so bad when there are others in here, too. But with you alone . . .

Well, you must admit you're no Johnny Carson, Mr. Morden. Not that you have to be. But neither should I have to waste ten counts . . . out of my life; counts that seem to go on for an eternity.

The choir of angels sings one chord.

MRS. BETHNAL-GREEN: So, it's a spanking new Otis for us. (*She waits for reaction from* MORDEN *but gets none.*) You *are* familiar with Otis. (*No response.*) Otis makes elevators. Otis makes just about the best elevators in the world, that's all. (*No response.*) There's an Otis in the Vatican.

The choir of angels sings one chord.

MORDEN: Will the new one have music?

MRS. BETHNAL-GREEN: Of course. Completely up-to-date.

MORDEN: I like music. Religious music, especially. Could never make the choir, though. Had to read music and I couldn't. So I became an altar boy, just to hear more of it.

MRS. BETHNAL-GREEN: Are you a murderer then, Mr. Morden?

MORDEN: What?

MORDEN'S VOICE (*off, echoing*): Bang! Bang! Bang! Bang!

MRS. BETHNAL-GREEN: Murderers—especially the ones who commit the most ghastly crimes—are often altar boys. Ergo . . .

MORDEN: Music will make it all very comfortable.

MRS. BETHNAL-GREEN: Not only music. Indirect lighting. And gorgeous, soft pastel paneling. Plastic, of course, for easy cleaning. And Otis will rise and fall swiftly, smoothly, and silently.

MORDEN: As if the walls in the elevator shaft had been greased up.

MRS. BETHNAL-GREEN: What?

MORDEN: As if a great mouth was at the bottom of the shaft.

And it was blowing this cage with such force that it took no effort at all to smash me right on through the roof.

The choir of angels sings one chord.

MRS. BETHNAL-GREEN: Mr. Morden, you're talking about death again, aren't you? You're being spooky and I won't have it. It's bad enough the doctor tries to scare me if I don't "behave." Well, he's a spook, too. And I won't cut out chocolates or anything else. In fact—look—now I'm going to cram this whole box of chocolate crunchy bars into my mouth. I was going to save some for watching the television later, but I'll just send out for more, lots more. That's the advantage of having money, Mr. Morden. You can send out at all hours for all the chocolates you want. Peanuts. Creamy fillings. Caramelos. Fruit and nut. Raisins. Jelly bars. More crunchies. Coconut and almond centers. The lot of them. I'll show all you spooks. You just keep your dying to yourself. (*Suddenly she clutches her throat, drops her candy bars and slumps over.*)

MORDEN: What is it, Mrs. Bethnal-Green?

MRS. BETHNAL-GREEN: Can't breathe . . . Hurry . . .

The choir of angels sings a chord which is sustained and held under.

MORDEN'S VOICE (*off, echoing*): Bang! Bang! Bang! (*The voice continues under the following.*)

MORDEN: It takes its own time. You know I can't.

MRS. BETHNAL-GREEN: Oh, please, please . . .

MORDEN: I would like to hurry, but . . .

MRS. BETHNAL-GREEN: Don't . . . don't do this to me, Mr. Morden . . .

MORDEN: There's nothing I can . . .

MRS. BETHNAL-GREEN: Please . . . I wasn't the only one . . . all the tenants voted for . . . Otis . . .

MORDEN: You run the goddamned building. Why couldn't

you just fix this one? *I* wanted one that would fly. I would have been content to stay in this cage forever if it could just fly . . .

MRS. BETHNAL-GREEN: . . . economical . . . economics . . .
Sound of whirring out. The elevator has stopped. All sounds out. Even in her pain, MRS. BETHNAL-GREEN *silently counts ten along with* MORDEN. *But the elevator doesn't start.*
Why doesn't it . . . start . . . ?

MORDEN (*frantically trying to get the elevator started*): I don't know. It never . . . (*He suddenly becomes excited.*) Yes. Yes, it did once.

In the distance, a soprano starts singing Bach's "Gott Versorget Alles Leben." Her singing grows louder during the following.

MORDEN: It stopped for a longer-than-ten count and stayed stopped for awhile. And when it started again, it went crazy. Shot up and down. Went wild, I remember. Picked up so much speed, you'd think it was going to fly right on through the—

MRS. BETHNAL-GREEN (*with all her strength*): Nooooooooooooooooooo! Don't say it, Mr. Morden! Help! Help!

MORDEN: What? . . . Oh, yes . . . My God, yes . . . (*Shouts.*) Help! Help! Mrs. Bethnal-Green, the Manager of this renovated building who is replacing me with an Otis automatic is very ill! Help! Help! (MORDEN *slides back one of the panels indented in the elevator's wooden wall. A priest, in profile to* MORDEN, *is on the other side.*)

FATHER UXBRIDGE: Yes, my son, I will help you, but you must calm down.

MORDEN: But I wanted to kill her, Father Uxbridge.

FATHER UXBRIDGE: Kill whom?

MORDEN: Debden, my lady friend.

FATHER UXBRIDGE: Why?

MORDEN: There's someone else. I know it.

FATHER UXBRIDGE: How do you know it?

MORDEN: She's out, away from her apartment, a lot more. Won't tell me where even though she knows I'm beside myself with jealousy.

FATHER UXBRIDGE: She goes out to work?

MORDEN: She works at home. Does typing. You see? There's no reason for her to go out that much. Then there's her eyes. I see it in her eyes. She's cheating, cheating, I know it.

FATHER UXBRIDGE: Calma, Morden. Calma. (*He rises and walks to the bench, stage right. His mask is round with flushed cheeks. It wears a perpetual, fatuous smile.*) One step at a time. You have agreed to go into this with me in some depth away from the sacred confessional. That's good. But we can only see things as they really are—only begin to get at the root of the problem—with less emotion. *Then* I'll help you. And you, Morden, will help me. First, come sit here (*he claps hands and* MORDEN *immediately rises, moves over to* UXBRIDGE *and sits, looking out over the audience*) and let us take a second or so—collect ourselves—by listening to the choir singer. An angelic voice. And singing divine music, Morden. Bach, Morden, Bach. (*Singing comes up, then quickly down.*) That's one change I'm grateful for. Bach, the Protestant. You weren't allowed to play him in the church at one time.

MORDEN (*showing real joy as he remembers the music*): I'd sit on the stairs and listen to the organist play Bach after the choir left. (*Now showing panic.*) One night the Pastor came back. Made a terrible scene about the music. Fired the organist right on the spot. The organist saw me after the Pastor left. Yelled at me like it was my fault. "You'll allow him, you'll see. Bach's said it all," he said. "Bach will have the last word."

FATHER UXBRIDGE: The words say that God provides for all the living.

MORDEN (*simply, just as a fact*): That's not what the music says.

FATHER UXBRIDGE (*taken aback*): Oh? And what does the music say about the living, Morden?

MORDEN (*simply, just as a fact*): That they all suffer.

Singing comes up, then down.

FATHER UXBRIDGE: And what else does the music say?

MORDEN: That it's sorry about it all.

Singing comes up for a second. UXBRIDGE *now listens to the music more intently. Music quickly brought down.*

MORDEN: It is nice. And so is she.

FATHER UXBRIDGE: Who?

MORDEN: The enamel girl.

FATHER UXBRIDGE: Enamel girl, Morden? What enamel girl?

The singing stops.

MORDEN (*with the simple joy of a pleasant memory*): We had a statue—a figurine, my mother called it—of a white angel. I said it was enamel because it felt good like the white enamel woodwork in the toilet. That was the one room where they'd let me be when I was a kid. So I'd sit there with my head resting against the white enamel woodwork. That figurine was really porcelain, but I always called it enamel.

FATHER UXBRIDGE: Morden, that's part of the trouble here. You see things in a strange way. And perhaps you're distorting this whole business with your lady friend.

MORDEN (*in a sudden murderous rage*): No. No. I'm not. Debden is cheating and I wanted to kill her and thinking of murder is a mortal sin.

FATHER UXBRIDGE: And you'll continue "thinking" of it as long as you continue this adulterous relationship with that woman.

MORDEN (*with real perplexity*): Adulterous? (*He has the answer.*) But Debden's a widow!

FATHER UXBRIDGE: But you're married.

MORDEN: I keep forgetting. (*He has the answer.*) But Stepney ran out on me such a long time ago.

FATHER UXBRIDGE: Still—in the eyes of the Church . . .

MORDEN (*confused*): But what could I do? (*He has the answer.*) Divorce is a sin, too.

FATHER UXBRIDGE: There are ways of getting around that problem. But until we do, there's only one course for you. Be chaste.

MORDEN: Chaste? Me? Well, you know, Father, I'm only a simple human being. I don't have the will power. I mean, I'm not endowed with that splendid light of God that gives you priests the strength to give it up. Not that there were many women before Debden. That's one of the reasons I need her so much. She's so—used to be so giving. But even before—even alone—sitting on the toilet in the enamel room—I mean, they used to say *that* made you go crazy. But that didn't stop me then, and wouldn't now. Do you see what I mean?

FATHER UXBRIDGE: "Chaste" was not the right word. I didn't mean you should lead a life of chastity, like a priest. No one would expect that of you. Indeed, the whole question of clerical chastity is now being debated, as you undoubtedly know. In fact, Morden, as Public Relations priest for this Parish, I'll be taping a television panel, probing just this subject. At the moment, I take a middle-of-the-road view of the matter. But one can see some justification for—

MORDEN: Priests? DOING IT? But that's disgusting! Sinful!

FATHER UXBRIDGE (*quickly, in the face of Morden's strong reaction*): You're absolutely right. When I say I take the middle-of-the-road view, I mean, as PR for this Parish I must be somewhat neutral. But I think I can confide in you that I veer toward the traditional view and . . .

MORDEN: I mean, if priests start doing it . . . Well, I don't know.

FATHER UXBRIDGE: The proponents, of course, play down fornication. Emphasize the marriage state.

MORDEN: Still . . .

FATHER UXBRIDGE: And the sacrament of marriage is what we're talking about re your problem. By chaste, I mean faithful to one spouse. I'll be vulgar. I mean, "doing it" with the blessings of the Church. That's the only way for you. Now, under certain circumstances you can divorce or get an annulment and remarry with our blessing. We would have to investigate thoroughly, but your case would seem to warrant such dispensation. Now, assuming this were possible, you would marry your lady friend.

MORDEN: No.

FATHER UXBRIDGE: Why not?

MORDEN: She wouldn't accept me.

FATHER UXBRIDGE: Why not?

MORDEN: She had a bad marriage. She's afraid to make it binding again.

FATHER UXBRIDGE: Then you must find someone else.

MORDEN: I couldn't.

FATHER UXBRIDGE: Why not?

MORDEN: Because . . . finding someone else . . . is . . .

FATHER UXBRIDGE: Yes?

MORDEN: . . . exhausting . . .

FATHER UXBRIDGE: So what? If this is important enough . . .

MORDEN: But women don't . . .

FATHER UXBRIDGE: Don't what?

MORDEN: . . . find me . . .

FATHER UXBRIDGE: Yes?

MORDEN: Good looking.

FATHER UXBRIDGE: Debden obviously found you attractive. Others will too.

MORDEN: It was different with her. She was in an accident. A crack up. I saw it. Her husband was driving. Only Debden and the child survived. I took care of them. Had some money then.

FATHER UXBRIDGE: Do you mean to say that your entire relationship has been built on her gratitude to you? And on your helping in a monetary way when you can afford it? Morden, aside from the problem of sin, you must bring it to a conclusion.

MORDEN: She came to care. She cares. And I love the little girl. (*There is the cry of a little girl, off.*) Angel! (ANGEL *rushes in.*) Angel, what's the matter? (ANGEL *does not wear a mask. She holds up a finger.*) You cut it. (*He sucks her finger and bandages it with his handkerchief.*) I told you to be careful with those scissors.

FATHER UXBRIDGE: Why did you allow the child to have the scissors? Why did you bring her here with you at all? And why doesn't she talk? Has the cat got her tongue?

MORDEN: She doesn't have a tongue. I mean, in a manner of speaking. The accident. It did something to her vocal cords. But she can hear. You should have seen her sitting still as a stick, listening with me to the enamel girl.

FATHER UXBRIDGE: There you go again with that enamel girl, Morden.

MORDEN: Anyway, there was no one home to leave her with. Debden went out (*whispers to* FATHER UXBRIDGE) do you see what I mean? (*In his normal voice.*) I had to take Angel with me. Besides, I wanted to.

ANGEL *makes a gesture of cutting with a scissors.*

FATHER UXBRIDGE: Does that mean she wants to use the scissors again?

MORDEN: Yes.

FATHER UXBRIDGE: You're not going to allow it!

MORDEN: Oh, I can't deny Angel anything. Anyway, besides listening to music, her cutouts are the only things that relax her. She loves to paste animal heads on pictures of people. (*He kisses her on the head.*) Go on back to your cutouts. But be careful. (ANGEL *runs off. He says the following simply.*) I love Angel. She's even more helpless than I am.

Pause.

FATHER UXBRIDGE: You're out of work now, eh?

MORDEN: Yes.

FATHER UXBRIDGE: I know of a job that's available.

MORDEN: I have few skills. That's one of my problems.

FATHER UXBRIDGE: A parishioner of mine manages an apartment building. At the moment she needs someone to run her elevator. You'd be able to run an elevator, eh, Morden?

MORDEN: I don't know. I'm not very mechanical. And I have funny reflexes.

FATHER UXBRIDGE: "Funny" reflexes?

MORDEN: I mean, I get tics. Like spasms in my muscles.

FATHER UXBRIDGE: Buttons, Morden. You just push buttons. Or manipulate one of those levers. Either/or. Push or manipulate, Morden. Push or manipulate.

MORDEN: And I'd have to meet people.

FATHER UXBRIDGE: Not meet, really. Just make sure they step on and off.

MORDEN: But, you see, I'm bound to have to look them in the eye at some point. I mean, those doors open and there they'll stand, staring before they enter.

FATHER UXBRIDGE: For a second, perhaps.

MORDEN: Oh, that's plenty of time. They'll stare as if they're blaming me.

FATHER UXBRIDGE: For what?

MORDEN: I don't know. But people always seem to be blaming somebody, and if I'm around, it's always me.

FATHER UXBRIDGE: Now, Morden . . .

MORDEN: The thought of it gives me the cramps, Father.

FATHER UXBRIDGE: The cramps?

MORDEN: Just thinking about a job always gives me the cramps. And during the first few weeks on the job, I always have the diarrhea. But mostly . . .

FATHER UXBRIDGE (*his patience nearing an end*) : I'll donate two weeks supply of Kaopectate!

MORDEN: But mostly I'm afraid of elevators.

FATHER UXBRIDGE: Afraid of what? Closed-in spaces?

MORDEN: No. That the bottom will drop out.

FATHER UXBRIDGE: Morden, I want you to take that job, do you hear? And I'll tell you why. (*He moves off quickly into the shadows for a moment and returns wheeling in a tape recorder. He switches the machine on and says the following into the machine's mike.*) Because I'm interested in the murderous soul, Morden. And I want to use you to illuminate a theory I have about it; the murderous soul. What I want to do is to eliminate all your superficial murder motives, Morden; bulldoze them out of your way and see what happens when you—simple, naïve, basic you—are left alone on the clear road to yourself. I suspect—hope—that murder will still stay stuck in your soul. For I have always seen the soul as made of cotton candy, for some strange reason; and in the shape of a mushroom cloud. And why that image, Morden? Because it's symbolic, of course. For what, after all, characterizes our time, Morden?—Violence. It seems to be the common denominator and may very well be at the heart of our age's soul. (*He switches the machine off.*) That's rather a nice phrase, eh, Morden?

MORDEN (*sings*): They've taken my Laddie away, O!
They've taken my Laddie away . . .

FATHER UXBRIDGE: Morden! Do I hear right. You're singing! I'm talking away and *you're* singing!

MORDEN: Oh. It just came to mind, Father. Part of a song my mother used to sing. I don't know why it came to me. I'm sorry.

FATHER UXBRIDGE: And indeed you should be. Now, are you going to pay attention or not?

MORDEN: Go on. Go on. Please, Father Uxbridge. I'm sorry. I really am.

FATHER UXBRIDGE: I lost my train of thought. (*He rewinds the tape. His voice, on tape, speaks.*) ". . . characterizes our time, Morden? Violence. It seems to be the common denominator and may very well be at the heart of our age's soul." (*He switches it off and clicks to record. He speaks into the mike.*) Violence. Oh, I suppose you would have said sex was the common denominator. On the surface, Morden. On the surface. Why, if you had heard what I have heard, you'd realize, too, that that today is violence, really. And you must believe me, Morden, I'm not against sex. It's a sacred gift from God. So sacred that it infuriates me to know that at any given moment on this planet—within the sacrament of marriage—a million dildoes are in use; not to mention the palsied hand. But that's another sermon.—Violence. And what's the logical extension of violence, Morden?—Murder, Morden. Do you think you're the only one grappling with murder? Oh, Morden, you have no idea what murderous thoughts are strained through that sieve separating confessor and confessed. But they all have—what shall I call it?—reasonable emotional excuses. Yes, they do. Even those just a few notches above your station, Morden. *They* have an excuse. They're being paid for less and less work and they don't know what to do with their leisure. Ergo: Dissatisfaction and boredom. Ergo: The pursuit of thrills—which means violence. Ergo: Again, murder, Morden.

MORDEN (*sings*): . . . they've taken my Laddie to string him up, O . . .

FATHER UXBRIDGE (*clicking machine off*): Morden! You're doing it again!

MORDEN: Sorry, Father. It's hard for me to concentrate long on anything. Especially when something intrudes like . . .

FATHER UXBRIDGE: That tune. Well, you will push that morbid song to the back of your fuzzy mind or by God, I'll . . . I'll EXCOMMUNICATE you. Now, listen! (*He rewinds the tape a bit. His voice, on tape, speaks.*) ". . . paid for less and less work and don't know what to do with their leisure. Ergo: Dissatisfaction and boredom. Ergo: The pursuit of thrills—which means violence. Ergo: Again, murder, Morden." (*He switches it off. Then he switches to record. He speaks into the mike.*)

But you, Morden . . . you're not even a member of a union that can get you a fantastic salary for not working. The most you'll ever reach, I would suspect, will be to live on the government dole. This would hardly lead to an affluence that could, as with the rest, lead to the boredom and dissatisfaction and so to the kind of violence I'm talking about. Yes, you'll always have the financial struggle and that struggle will ward off the boredom. You won't have that excuse. But we might still find that, at base, once you're free of the Debden problem and you have the elevator job, there will still be murder in your soul. At base. At base. There's the key, Morden. To wrench out—scientifically—the basics from a basic. That's you, Morden.

FATHER UXBRIDGE:	MORDEN:
	A guinea pig?
A primitive who will help us get down to es- sentials and fast.	Is that what you want to use me for, Father? Some kind of guinea pig?
Yes, we must strip away all your . . .	No. No. I'm through with all that.

MORDEN: I mean, I'm tired of it; all my life a guinea pig. The kids on the block—in school. Even in the army. You know what they did once—my buddies? There was this big lunk of a guy in our barracks who stank; stank like strong cheese. And they all wanted to scrub him. They had these big horse-hair brushes and strong brown soap and when a guy stank they'd just scrub the skin off him. But this particular guy who stank like cheese was strong as a tank, you see, and no one would take him on. So I'm taking a shower one day, filthy from having cleaned the grease pit and, on the garbage truck, from having been up to my ankles in thrown-out string beans and shit-on-a-shingle, when this gorilla grabs me in the shower and says, "So you're going to scrub me?" Then he throws me up against the wall, brushes my skin until I bleed and beats me up to boot. Breaks two ribs and gives me a kidney condition. What happened was, my "buddies" told him that I would do it. Why? Some of them took bets on how fast he could take me. But all of them hoped the gorilla would hurt me real bad so that he'd be thrown out of the barracks. Well, that's just what happened. While I was in the hospital, he was transferred and . . . Oh, God, I'm sorry, Father. I didn't mean to say shit-on-a . . . I mean that army word for chipped beef on toast. But that's what happens when you talk guinea pig. I mean, that's pretty cruel, if that's what you think I am. Because I'm not. Not anymore. I'm no guinea pig.

Pause.

FATHER UXBRIDGE: Forgive me, Morden. I didn't mean to be cruel. Or did I? That is, after all, the fashion, isn't it? You see, things are changing. Did you know, Morden, that jazz has been allowed into the Mass? And a Catholic priest recently addressed the Masons? Why, if this keeps up, one of these days I may even have to address the Jesuits. (*Crosses himself.*) God forbid. (*Tired laugh.*) Change . . . Change? Upheaval. And in this upheaval, others—younger ones are moving in. Why, there's even a rumor that I may be replaced here. A certain Father Ongar . . . is . . . creating . . . favorable static in upper clerical circles.

FATHER ONGAR *appears. In the background, a brief mysterious musical chord.* FATHER ONGAR *wears a smoothly white, characterless mask.*
Every so often, throughout the following, FATHER UXBRIDGE *looks over his shoulder sensing someone behind him. But* FATHER ONGAR *moves aside deftly.*

FATHER UXBRIDGE: So, Morden, one tries to hold on. To survive. How? By having a thing—a schtick, our Hebrew brethren would call it. And I may quote them freely now. Indeed, must, in this—Ecumenical Era . . . The murderous soul. That's my schtick. And I really believe that you—especially you—can help me.

FATHER ONGAR *throws back his head as if he's laughing. He wheels the tape recorder off into the shadows.*

MORDEN: But can you help me? That's what I'm here for. I mean, I see you're hot on this murder thing . . . I don't understand it . . . but o.k. But what about me and Debden and Angel . . .

FATHER UXBRIDGE: In the process, Morden . . . in the process, we can get you squared away. Everything is connected, Morden. But we've got to dig—reach out in many directions to find . . . (*Pause.*) The simple fact is—I'm losing it. Something is slipping away, Morden—and I'm frightened. Morden, please work with me. That's right. We'll work together. Probe together. And together pray to God that we do find that the soul is at base a murderous one. Something that negative would really delight them all.

MORDEN: And what will I have to do?

FATHER UXBRIDGE: Just talk, Morden. To me. Oh, sometimes, perhaps, I'll use you as illustration during one of my talks. But I'll make that painless. I'm a very good lecturer, Morden. Also—yes—I don't see why I can't manage to scrape up some petty cash for you—for your contribution. Now, how does that sound?

MORDEN: And what about my invalid mother?

FATHER UXBRIDGE: What *about* your invalid mother?

MORDEN: I'm not free of her.

FATHER UXBRIDGE: Hm . . . We can place her—in a good Catholic nursing home for our Senior Souls.

MORDEN: Charity?

FATHER UXBRIDGE: Christian charity, Morden. Nothing to be ashamed of.

FATHER ONGAR *wheels on* MORDEN'*s* MOTHER, *who is in a wheelchair. Her mask is chalk white, non-smiling, with sunken cheeks and deep eye sockets.* FATHER ONGAR *places the chair so that the* MOTHER *faces* MORDEN.

MORDEN (*looking away*): I don't know. Is it right?
FATHER UXBRIDGE: If it's an unreasonable burden on you, it is. (FATHER ONGAR *hands the wheelchair over to* FATHER UXBRIDGE.) Why, the handing over of mothers is a common occurrence today.
MOTHER'S VOICE (*over*): Bed sores.
MORDEN: What about bed sores?
FATHER UXBRIDGE: What *about* bed sores?

FATHER UXBRIDGE *hands the wheelchair back to* FATHER ONGAR, *then moves downstage with his back to the audience.* FATHER ONGAR, *upstage center, keeps the* MOTHER *facing* MORDEN, *who looks out over the audience.*

MORDEN: She used to say . . . (*He moves his lips but we hear the* MOTHER'*s voice.*)
MOTHER'S VOICE (*over*): You'll see, my son. Someday, when I'm used up, you'll put me in a hospital or a home. And they won't bother with me there. They'll let me get bed sores and I'll just rot away. And that'll be my thanks for bringing you up alone when your father ran out on me.
MORDEN: She used to call it "running out on her." His dying. The poor bastard got all mangled up in a machine. Funny she never blamed God.
FATHER UXBRIDGE: God, Morden? You mean the Angel of Death. At any rate, we'll make sure she finds herself in a friendly home, professionally looked after . . .
MORDEN: She used to say . . .
MOTHER'S VOICE: You'll put me in a nursing home and you'll agonize about it, but you'll do it anyway. Because, for one thing, it won't be pretty. Don't I know? Didn't I

take care of my vegetable mother? And didn't I hand her over to the State? Vegetable mothers run in our family, Morden. I must tell you that. But then there's the other—deeper—reason for pushing vegetable mother out. By then you'll reach the point where you'll want to get even for being cheated, and I'll be convenient to get even on. Oh, yes. Oh, yes. In a rage, someday, you'll push me out. I know you will—but I hope you won't. And I tell you this now in the hope that at that moment, when you're ready to push me out, you'll remember what I'm saying and maybe you'll show compassion and keep me with you . . . Morden, I think I've done my best by you. But sometimes there were forces that— But, listen, remember when you were little and laid up in the clinic with rheumatic fever? I'd put the alcohol-soaked rag on your forehead and I'd sing you the lullaby you loved. When you go to push me out, think of this. (*Sings.*)
Go to sleep, my baby.
The sun will not peep through.
Dark, dark, dark all night.
Dark all day, too.

FATHER ONGAR *has moved away and stands in the shadows.* MORDEN *goes to the wheelchair. He avoids looking into the Mother's face.*

MORDEN: No. No. It's out of the question, Father. (*He begins wheeling the chair around.*) I mean—a son's duty. It's the least I can do after all the pain she went through for me. I mean, so what if I have to change her soiled diaper? Didn't she change mine when I was a kid? Oh, yes, kid-soiled is cute, while grown-up-soiled gets you sick. But that's a small price to pay for all she sacrificed. And so what if her moans—they're the only sounds she makes, you know—so what if those moans become stuck in your head? (*He's wheeling faster. Sound of moans, amplified.*) And you carry them around like bees in your ears all day. So what if Debden won't come to the house because she can't stand the sight and smell of rotting mother?—No. Not bees. It's more like a car idling, those moans. Idling, all day long. Low hum, all day long, with never the hope of acceleration. Well, so what if you never have the voom-Voom-VOOM of acceleration? Where are you going? Where's there to go to? Why does it have to be voom-Voom-VOOM? So what if the care you're giving makes no sense because God—I mean the Angel of Death—is going to take her anyway, bed sores or not—even though it might take years? So what if it's like looking into the mirror of death every time I look at her and I know that that low moan idling hum is going to buzz on until I go off my head? Huh? So what? No. No. I can't push her out.

He has aimed the wheelchair at the audience and given it a shove. Just as the wheelchair gets to the apron, FATHER UXBRIDGE *steps out and stops it.*

FATHER UXBRIDGE: Yes. It's the only way. The best way for her. (*He takes the wheelchair from* MORDEN *and wheels it off into the shadows.* MORDEN *stands looking out over the audience.*) And you, Morden, when you start to work and when you deal with the Debden problem, you'll be free to be yourself and then we'll see about the murder in your soul, Morden. Deal with Debden, Morden.

Pause.

MORDEN (*suddenly aware he's alone*): Angel! Angel! ANGEL! I need you. (FATHER ONGAR *pushes her out and disappears back into the shadows.* MORDEN *rushes to her and hugs her violently.*) You're still here. You'll never leave me, Angel? Right? I won't let you. (ANGEL *cries.*) What's the matter? Oh, I frightened you. That's from love, Angel. Do you understand? My love frightened you. Here . . . a song . . . Would you like to hear a song? I remember it now. (*Sings.*)
They've taken my Laddie away, O.

They've taken my Laddie away.
They've taken my Laddie to string him up, O.
He's going to Great Fall Hill.
Scream, my Laddie, kick on the wind,
No one will listen but me.
Oh, as they drag you up Great Fall Hill,
No one will listen but me.

ANGEL *tries to get him to leave, but he is lost in the song.* FATHER ONGAR *enters and makes a scissors sign.* ANGEL *runs to him. They exit.*

They've taken my Laddie away, O.
They've taken my Laddie away.
They've taken my Laddie to string him up, O.
He's going to Great Fall Hill.

MRS. BETHNAL-GREEN *moans.*

Father Uxbridge, Mother's gone, but the moans stay.

MRS. BETHNAL-GREEN (*in the elevator*) : Mr. Morden.

MORDEN *walks to the elevator as the soprano sings Bach's "Hört, ihr Augen, auf zu weinen."*

MRS. BETHNAL-GREEN (*weaker than ever*) : Mr. Morden . . .

The singing is down very low.

MORDEN: Shh. Shh! The enamel girl next door. She's practicing again. Drives Stepney crazy when the enamel girl stops and starts.

MRS. BETHNAL-GREEN: Enamel gi— . . . Stepney . . . Dear God . . . he's gone crazy.

MORDEN: If we're lucky, she'll sing right through, Mrs. Bethnal-Green. Then—Green! Isn't that strange. That was Stepney's maiden name. Stepney Green, my wife who ran out on me.

FATHER ONGAR (*from above, off*) : Morden! Mrs. Bethnal-Green!

MRS. BETHNAL-GREEN (*weakly*) : Oh . . . help . . .

FATHER ONGAR (*off*) : . . . Do you hear me?
MORDEN (*whispering to* MRS. BETHNAL-GREEN) : Shh. I know the voice.
FATHER ONGAR (*off*) : Can you hear me?
MORDEN : It's the anti-Christ and fornicator.
FATHER ONGAR (*off*) : It's Father Ongar.
MRS. BETHNAL-GREEN (*with all her strength*) : Oh, help! Help!
MORDEN : Shh!
FATHER ONGAR (*off*) : I hear you, Mrs. Bethnal-Green. Are you all right?
MORDEN : What are you doing here? How did you know about this?
FATHER ONGAR (*off*) : Just administered last rites. Someone's dying.
MORDEN : A woman, I'll bet. Did you fornicate her?
FATHER ONGAR (*off*) : Morden, I'm coming down.
MORDEN : How?
FATHER ONGAR (*off*) : The cable.
MORDEN (*to* MRS. BETHNAL-GREEN) : Showing off his strength. That's for your benefit.
MRS. BETHNAL-GREEN : Don't care. I want him. I want him.
MORDEN : Do you hear that, Father Ongar? Mrs. Bethnal-Green wants you. Does that mean you're going to do it to her right here in front of me? Like you did to Debden?
MRS. BETHNAL-GREEN : Oh, dear God . . .
FATHER ONGAR (*off*) : Morden, I'm coming down.
MORDEN : Save your strength, Father Ongar. All we can do is wait it out—until it makes up its mind to—soar! Maybe smash right on through the roof!
FATHER ONGAR (*off*) : Morden, I said I'm coming down.
MORDEN : Then I won't let you through the trap. (*He stands on tip toes, reaches up, and holds down the handle of the trap. The soprano starts singing again.*) Oh, she's starting again. If she starts and stops now, Stepney will hit the roof.
MRS. BETHNAL-GREEN (*crawling to* MORDEN, *face down*) :

Morden . . . I'll give you money . . . two months' severance pay . . . three . . .

The soprano stops singing.

MORDEN: She stopped . . . (*The soprano starts again.*) She's starting again . . . (*From this point until indicated, the soprano starts and stops singing, as if practicing the piece.*) Now there'll be hell to pay.

MRS. BETHNAL-GREEN (*still face down*): Morden . . . please . . . I can't . . . I . . .

She lifts her face; she now has on another mask, the mask of . . .

STEPNEY GREEN (*rising*): I can't stand this! (*She runs out of the elevator to the center stage area.*)

MORDEN: Stepney!

Stepney Green's mask is contorted, as if her face had been frozen at the precise moment of a severe gastric attack.

STEPNEY GREEN (*stamping on the floor*): Stop it! Stop that singing! Stop iiiiiiiiiiiiiiit! (*The singing continues.*) Morden, she won't stop. Now, you go right downstairs and force her to stooooooooooooop!

Throughout this scene, MORDEN *stays in the elevator and answers* STEPNEY GREEN *from there.*

MORDEN: Stepney, I can't. My ugly hands. My psoriasis.

STEPNEY GREEN: You're wearing gloves. She won't know.

MORDEN: But *I* know. *I* know.

STEPNEY GREEN: Your psoriasis. Your arthritis. Your foot fungus. Keep you from jobs. They fire you because of all that. Well, I don't care. I keep my job. Christ! Even your mother keeps her's. Sorry now I threw the nag out. She at least would have talked that croaking bitch to death right through the floor . . . Morden, will you listen to that! I work hard all day, I tell you. And I don't want to hear that screeching when I come home. All I want is to watch my television. And I don't want to watch it through thaaaaaaaaaaaat! Morden, it's your job. Stop her. Because if I go downstairs I'll cut her vocal cords; choke her by stuffing all her music down her throat; bang her metronome through her skull like a spike. I'll do something mean, I mean it. Meeeeeeaaaaaan it! (*The singing stops.*) Thank you, Miss Screech. (*She walks into the shadows.*) Now I'll just switch on the television good and loud. (*She wheels in a television set and switches it on. A light reflects on her face as the TV set lights up. Suddenly there's a little explosive sound in the set. She begins switching dials frantically. She puts her head to the set as if listening for a heartbeat.*) Morden! It's dead! I told you the tube was weak. I told you to take it in! God, you're worthless. Why? Why did I ever marry you? Why did you ever marry me? Oh, what's the difference? It's broken. Stopped dead. Is—not—working! Will—not—utter—sound! Won't—make—picture! Do you understand that, Morden? (*She pushes the set viciously into the shadows.*) Do you know what that means? It's Saturday night. You won't get anyone until Monday. *If* you're lucky. I might be without a television until Tuesday. Or Wednesday! Four whole nights—with nothing! NOTHING! Do you hear, you—you itchy fungus, you! It's dead! DEAD! Morden! *Now what?*

The singing begins again. STEPNEY GREEN *turns her back to the audience, screams, and covers her ears with her hands. Lights out on* STEPNEY GREEN.

In the elevator, MORDEN *has his hands over his ears. The singing stops and he slowly takes his hands away from his ears.*

Lights up on STEPNEY GREEN *again. When she turns around to face the audience, she's . . .*

DEBDEN: "Sometimes there's a terrible scream inside."

Debden's mask is sad, the checks hollow. One cheek has a vicious scar. She walks into the shadows and wheels in a cart with a suitcase on it. She recites as she packs.

MORDEN (*from the elevator*) : Debden.

DEBDEN : "Why couldn't God make me the type to get that scream out?"

MORDEN (*from the elevator*) : Debden.

DEBDEN : "It would be such a satisfying scream. Long . . . sustained . . . full of rocks and sand and broken glass . . . ripping . . . burning . . . forcing me to spit up blood, perhaps, but that couldn't stop it. Even if my throat was being ripped out by that scream, that scream wouldn't stop."

MORDEN (*from the elevator*) : Debden.

DEBDEN : "A monumental scream. A scream to end all screams. And it would yank out—drag out—wriggling, like tin cans and obscenities—my heart, liver, uterus, bones, and breath. Finally cleaning me out; leaving me a limp, wrinkly skin; some huge, punctured, mustard-colored balloon, shriveled in the dirt."

DEBDEN (*picking up a sheet of paper*) : That was from a play I wrote, Morden. Self-indulgent. All monologue, as I recall. Still, I won a prize for that play in my undergraduate days. I was considered quite a writer. With a brilliant future. (*She rips up the paper.*) Curtain. (*She lets the pieces flutter to the floor.*)

MORDEN (*from the elevator*) : Debden.

DEBDEN (*picking up a hand mirror*) : How is it possible for a woman my age to have acne?

MORDEN (*leaving the elevator*) : Debden, don't leave me.

DEBDEN : My period has never been regular. My mother had beautiful skin. I guess her's was.

MORDEN : Debden, your face has a scar and you limp.

DEBDEN *drops the mirror.*

DEBDEN: No! (*She limps away, then moves about.*)

MORDEN: You were in an accident that left you with a scar and a limp. I took care of you. If you leave me, no one else will.

DEBDEN: Don't be cruel, Morden. Please. I'm trying to face reality. But don't make me face it all at once, I'm not strong enough for that. Not yet.

MORDEN: I don't want to be cruel, but what about me? What will I do if you leave me?

DEBDEN: You'll do what you always do; exist . . . Oh, Morden, I'm sorry. I didn't mean that. Well, I mean I did mean that, but I didn't mean it to sound so bitter. I'll try it another way . . . You'll do what you always do . . . (*with compassion*) . . . exist.

MORDEN: At least tell me who he is.

DEBDEN: There are no villains. Sometimes there are no villains.

MORDEN: There's got to be someone.

DEBDEN: There were people who believed in me. Morden, I've got to get involved with my own kind again. I've sat here feeling sorry for myself, allowing you to take care of me . . .

MORDEN: . . . *and* Angel! I've taken care of her, too. Don't forget that. Or have you even thought about her? What about her? You're not taking her?

DEBDEN (*calls*): Angel! (*To* MORDEN:) She's mine. Of course I'm taking her. (*Calls.*) Angel! (*To* MORDEN:) I'll provide for her. (*Calls.*) Angel, put those scissors away and come help Mommy pack.

MORDEN: Provide? (FATHER ONGAR *pushes* ANGEL *in.*) Oh, I see. Once away from me, you'll be free to go about your "business."

DEBDEN: Oh, no . . . not that again.

MORDEN: Bring your customers right to the house.

DEBDEN: Angel, come here. Don't listen!

FATHER ONGAR *rushes* ANGEL *over to* DEBDEN. DEBDEN

covers Angel's ears with Angel's own hands. FATHER ONGAR *exits.*

MORDEN: I have seen it. Haven't I visited such filthy bitches? Haven't I been taken on right under the same roof with the bitch's kid? And sooner or later the kid becomes useful. That's what Angel's going to be—Mommy's little helper . . .

DEBDEN (*showing her wrists*): Morden, I tried to kill myself! Are you trying to make me do it again?

DEBDEN *sobs.* MORDEN *rushes to her, falls to his knees, and kisses one bandaged wrist.*

MORDEN: Mommy's hurt, Angel. You, too. You kiss the hurt.

They both kiss her bandaged wrists.

DEBDEN: Morden, Morden, let us go.

MORDEN: Why did you do this, Debden? Why?

DEBDEN: I'm a witch, Morden. I can make people die by wanting it badly enough. Just before the car accident, I knew I wanted my husband to die. And he did. And I never stopped blaming myself. Now—lately—I've been feeling the same about you. And I despaired . . .

MORDEN: Jesus, Debden. That's a terrible sin. I mean, no matter how bad it all is, you should never try to kill yourself. No, no, no, you're staying. Angel, you and me—we'll take care of Mommy, because Mommy isn't strong enough to go . . .

DEBDEN: Not strong? (*She pulls away.*) I wasn't when I tried this. But I've since had some expert guidance. Now I know that I have a right to live, Morden. No matter how hurt you are, I have a right to leave, if I choose. And I do choose. I'm going, Morden.

MORDEN: What expert guidance? . . . No, you can't . . . I won't . . . Angel, you agree with me. Right? And you want to stay here with me, don't you? (ANGEL *nods.*) You see, Debden. She wants to stay with me.

DEBDEN: Angel, you want to be with Mommy wherever she goes, don't you? (ANGEL *runs to her mother, nodding.*) All right, dear. Go play until we're ready to leave.

ANGEL *goes off into the shadows. Pause.*

MORDEN: Don't take Angel away from me. I know she's not really my child, but she's become mine. And—I don't know how I know this, but—I'll never have a child of my own. Debden, don't take her away. Things are good now. My mother's gone, my old marriage has been annulled and I'm working. There—there—that's the main thing. I've got a steady job and I *can* provide.

DEBDEN: Not for long.

MORDEN: What?

DEBDEN: They're replacing you with an automatic elevator.

MORDEN: How do you know? I didn't know that. Where did you hear that, huh?

DEBDEN: At the rectory.

MORDEN: Father Uxbridge. But you only met him once. With me.

DEBDEN: I've been back.

MORDEN: Why? You didn't even like him.

DEBDEN: No, but there was no one else and I had to talk to someone.

MORDEN: What did he tell you?

DEBDEN: Nothing.

MORDEN: What did he tell you?

DEBDEN: Nothing. I only saw him once. When I went back the next time, he was giving a lecture. I looked in. Saw you sitting on a stool.

MORDEN: I got money for that. Anyway, I don't go anymore. But *you* went back. Why? Why?

DEBDEN: I had to talk to someone. I called Father Uxbridge again. But he was leaving. They were sending him on a lecture tour. Something about "the new clergy."

MORDEN: New. Yes. New's right. You knew then and you know now.

DEBDEN: What?
MORDEN: That Father Uxbridge wants to marry.
DEBDEN: No.
MORDEN: You must have. Everyone knew. That's why I stopped seeing him. Disgusting.
DEBDEN: He advocates marriage for priests? So what? A lot do now.
MORDEN: I don't care what a lot of 'em advocate. *He* wants to marry. That's the upsetting thing. There was an article—in a magazine. By a Father X. Well, it didn't take some of the ladies in the Parish long to figure out who Father X was. Mrs. Bethnal-Green herself—yes, my employer—high up in the Church because of her donations—herself, reached that conclusion. Uxbridge—even the first time I talked to him, he talked about it. Then he had no opinion, he said. Then he said he took the middle road. The middle road—sure. Right to a lady's middle. I'll bet he was after yours.
DEBDEN: I only saw him once. And Father Ongar . . .
MORDEN: Who?
DEBDEN: The priest I've been seeing.
MORDEN: Ongar? I know that name. What about him?
MORDEN'S VOICE (*over*): Bang, bang, bang, bang, bang . . .

The sound crescendoes under the following.

DEBDEN: My counselor . . . He replaced Father Uxbridge.
MORDEN: And this Father Ongar, he wants to get at your middle.
DEBDEN: Nobody wants to get at my middle.
MORDEN: I do. I do. What about that. I need it. What will I do without it?
DEBDEN: There'll be others. There are always others.
MORDEN: No. There won't be. Anyway, I want you.
DEBDEN: But I don't want you . . .
MORDEN: Suddenly! Suddenly!
DEBDEN: No. Yes. What's the difference. Now I know.
MORDEN: What?

DEBDEN: That you're beneath me!

"Bang, bang, bang," brought down very low. The sound crescendoes again under the following.

FATHER ONGAR *enters. He moves in front of* DEBDEN *and faces* MORDEN. DEBDEN *turns so that she's standing back to back with* FATHER ONGAR.

DEBDEN: I know it's cruel. But sometimes you've got to be cruel. It's over, Morden. We're through. I've found others who aren't—beneath me; whom I can look up to—stretch my mind up to. Morden, my brain has atrophied with you.

MORDEN: You scarred cripple! Beneath you! Who told you to think that? This new one? This Father Ongar? (FATHER ONGAR *quickly moves aside and* DEBDEN *turns to face* MORDEN.) I could kill you! Kill you! God, isn't it right to kill that cruelty? I'll bet there's something in The Book that gives you that o.k. You're smart, Debden. Quote me something from The Book.

DEBDEN: Please, Morden! . . .

MORDEN: There must be something. When they nailed Him to the cross. No. That part forgives. Some part that gives me the right to . . .

DEBDEN: Morden, don't do anything to me, please . . .

The "bangs" quieten.

MORDEN: No. I won't do anything to you, because this is how it's going to be. You're going to stay here and you can have all the customers you want—here. Right in this house. You can diddle away here for the rest of your life. I don't care. Just as long as you diddle me once in a while. And I don't even care anymore if you keep on laying stiff as a stick under me . . . But I'll take care of Angel. I'll give her all my love. I'll be her father and mother. Because no slut should be. Agreed?

The sound of banging crescendoes again.

DEBDEN: No! (*Shouts.*) Angel! (*To* MORDEN:) No! (FATHER ONGAR *pushes* ANGEL *in. He quickly moves back into the shadows.*) Come on, darling. We're going now.

MORDEN *grabs* ANGEL.

MORDEN: You're not taking her anywhere.

FATHER ONGAR *returns with the scissors and places them in Morden's hand. He raises Morden's hand.*

DEBDEN: Morden!
MORDEN: She's mine. I love her so much I'll kill her rather than let her go.

FATHER ONGAR *makes a gesture. The sound of "Bang, bang, bang" comes up very loud.*

DEBDEN: Don't, Morden. (*She screams.*)

MORDEN *lets* ANGEL *go.*

MORDEN: How can I kill her with so much noise? And it's getting worse. (FATHER ONGAR *takes the scissors from* MORDEN. *He exits.* MORDEN *covers his ears. The "bangs" stop.*) The thing is, it had stopped. You know? All the while I was sure of you. Now . . . wait . . . A movie . . . Once I saw this movie . . they had a scene . . . I think it was a movie . . . maybe I dreamed it? . . . Anyway, in it, they were nailing Him to the cross. And the thing about it, you see, was that the men doing the nailing were simple fellows, you know. Carpenters, I guess. That sort. And they're chatting like you do when you work together with someone all the time. You know? And I remember that one of them keeps a large—very large—nail in his teeth all the while he's talking. And at the same time he's talking—with that nail in his teeth—he's arranging the arm, you see. Straightening it out on the cross and forcing open the hand. Palm up . . . And that's something in itself. You can't see his face; the one who's being nailed,

I mean. But he's putting up a struggle. You can tell that by the way those two fellows are having trouble keeping his arm straight and the palm open, face up. In fact—yes—one of them has to put his knee on the arm to keep it down. And you figure, that's strange because he knows there's nothing he can do about it, the one who's being nailed, I mean. In fact, he's known it all along. Even before he was born. Right? In fact, that's what he was born for. But that doesn't seem to matter. I mean, from the struggle he's making, you can see that he doesn't want to die. Imagine? . . . Anyway, the one with the nail between his teeth takes it out. Looks at it. It's a shiny, new nail. He looks around, puts the shiny one in his pocket and takes out an old, rusty one. "Sure. What the hell," the other one—his friend—says. "Why waste a new one?" Then he looks at the palm—face up—and he places the old, rusty nail right smack in the center of that face-up palm and the beam right underneath that palm—just with his eye. And bang! One fast shot and the nail is through. But it's messy. I mean, blood spurting out all over. And that's a shock, too. In all the pictures where you saw the hole in the palm, I remembered it was always clean. Neat. Just a little round shaft from front to back. Oh, maybe a little blood just around the rim. But neat. Dried and neat. But here—Well, when you stop to figure it, the nail *has* to smash through veins and little bones and arteries before it catches in the wood. I mean, in true life where there's pain, it does . . . Anyway, there's this funny little part where fingers on the face-up palm jerk in. You know, like a reflex to cover the hurt as soon as the nail tears through. And the carpenter gets annoyed. And so he makes a face—a funny face, the carpenter does, as if to say, "Dear God, all I want to do is my job and look at this! There's no cooperation." So what he does is, he pries back the fingers and begins to hammer down the rusty nail in the center of that face-up palm into the wooden beam . . . And that's when it happened to me . . . Throughout the whole thing, I was pretty much out of it. I mean—oh—it was terrible and all, but I really couldn't side with any of them. You never saw his face, the one who was being nailed, I mean. And the carpenters . . . well, I guess they were too skilled for me to really feel any kinship with. But I was there somewhere. I knew that. And you know where? You know *what* I was in that scene? I was the bangs! (*The sound of "Bang, bang, bang . . ." begins again.*) I suddenly recognized the sound. Those bangs. My voice. Those bangs were my voice. My voice was those bangs. And you know how they do in movies. They turn up the sound. Bang, bang, bang! My voice banging away at that rotten nail into the face-up palm! I thought they'd all recognize me, those people sitting in the movie house. And the one thing I wanted more than ever at that moment was to be an invisible giant; go up to that screen with a giant knife, stab it at the top and hack down. Then stab it at the side and slash across. Then rip those flapping sections right out of that mouth, forever opened and black, and I looked down in it after slashing out that silver membrane and got dizzy, dizzy. The invisible giant was about to fall in nothing. Debden! (*The "bangs" stop.*) Debden? . . . Angel? (*He frantically looks around.*) Debden! . . . Debden! . . . (*Pause. He sees Debden's mask and picks it up.*) You used to like it when I dipped my fingers in the ice cube tray and touched your burning scar. (*Pause.*) Father Ongar! Ongar! I'll kill him.

MORDEN *flings the mask into the shadows as* FATHER ONGAR *enters.*

FATHER ONGAR: Before we start, I wonder if you'd mind assisting me in a little demonstration, Mord?

MORDEN: My name is Morden, Father Ongar.

FATHER ONGAR: Right. Now, if you'll just stand—there.

MORDEN: Well, I don't know. Will it . . . ?

FATHER ONGAR: It won't hurt you. It's designed to hurt them

. . . First—arms at your side . . . Now, cross your right hand over to the bend in your left arm . . . Left arm! Left arm! Right to left . . . That's correct. Now, raise your left arm from the elbow and cover your left eye with the palm of your left hand . . . No, no. Palm against your left eye. Left, left! . . . Keep your left elbow against your left rib cage . . . Now, bend your knees a bit and look like you're in the midst of a cramp. Not bad. That look sort of comes natural to you, doesn't it? But not good enough. Tell you what: Think of something terrible—really terrible for you. C'mon. C'mon. (*The sound of "Bang, bang, bang!"*) Good. (*The sound stops.*) You've lost it. What happened?

MORDEN: It was—too painful thinking of that.

FATHER ONGAR: Well, then think of something else. Out loud. Say it out loud and that will make it easier.

Pause.

MORDEN: I'm ashamed to admit it, Father, but I've never gotten over being afraid of the dark. I mean—in the dark—I get the feeling the floor will—end. And there'll be a long . . . drop . . . So, I have to stand frozen in one spot if I'm alone. Because if I move, I—may—Sometimes I get on my hands and knees. Inch along the floor to the lamp, feeling in front of me . . .

FATHER ONGAR: The abyss. You fear the abyss. I understand. (*He makes a gesture and the lights go out.*) It's dark now, Morden, and you dasn't move else (*imitates a falling scream*) heeeeeeeeeeeeeeelp! . . . Now, while you stand there terrified, I'll practice my sermon. *Don't move,* I said . . . (*He makes a gesture and the electronic music begins. He lights a candelabra of four or five candles and places it so that it causes a flickering shadow of* MORDEN *in his palm-to-eye, crouching position to appear upstage.*) My brethren. Michelangelo Buonarotti, that clever wop fairy, painted a vision of the last judgment in which some of humanity, surprised—but not too put out for, after all, *they* had it made—are allowing themselves to be hoisted up to a glorious heaven in the arms of muscular angels. While others, frightened as only those who glimpse an eternity of suffering *can* be frightened, are reluctantly being dragged down to the piss hole of hell . . . To me, the center of that stormy scene is the figure called "the condemned sinner." (*He points to* MORDEN.) In this tableau, we see a rendering of this unfortunate man. What are missing here, of course, are the demons and serpents gleefully dragging him down. There's one serpent—a real charmer—with its jaw clamped to the thigh, ready to chomp. You must imagine, too, the victim without his clothes. Now, why do I say that this figure is really the center of this turbulent scene? Because the rest is cheap theatrics. The apocalypse as seen by Cecil B. DeMille or John Huston. But in this one figure; in the amazed, frightened, hurt, verge-of-hysteria look is something profoundly recognizable. What, I wonder? (*Pause.*) Why, it's none other than our soul itself, my brethren—made concrete, peeking at its moment-before-conscious damnation. Why does he peek? Some have amusingly suggested that he only has one eye, that there is just an empty socket there—or just skin. Others have said that in place of eyeball or socket is a hideous boil that the artist, after he had painted it, was too squeamish to have us see, or that some Pope forced the artist to hide. There are all sorts of interpretations, none of which makes sense to me. Why *does* he peek? Weeell, he can't look because it's too horrible. So he covers one eye. But he must look because he can't believe it. For certainly in that look is the pained, eternal why? Why, the one eye is saying to God, are you punishing me when you've made the course compulsory? . . . There's something else in that look, of course. The shock of recognition. The recognition that God is cruel and the New Testament a phony, devised by some pansy historians with no balls. Sugar-coating PR men who put us on, their descendants continuing to do so. The truth being that we *are* made in God's image and so God is venal, spiteful, and craves revenge; must get even, as must we all. And there he stands (*points to* MORDEN), victim of God's revenge; the God who made him and steered him to damnation. (*He makes a gesture and the music stops. A change of tone.*) That's as far as I've gotten. I'll develop this theme of the need for getting even and build to the conclusion that God is really cruel and so, to understand and love Him, we must be cruel as well. And I have a fancy notion to put a period on it all by serving the congregation sugar cubes in lieu of the wafer. We'll annihilate the past—for we've got to find our own way to His cruelty—by going on a psychedelic trip. I, leading the way, of course. And the whole church will be a Chagall world. I'll put red velvet on all the walls and everyone, in their Sunday froufrou, will float fapitzt in a blue-green haze. (*To* MORDEN:) Watch it, Mord, you'll collide with my organ. (MORDEN *ducks and covers his head.* FATHER ONGAR *blows out the candles and the stage lights come up. He places the candelabra in the shadows during the following.*) And then, when I've tuned up their nervous systems to a pitch that only dogs can hear; and when their selfishness—that is, their need for instant gratification—has been developed to an exquisite degree, they'll be ready for my master plan . . . I'll reintroduce sacrifices into the ritual. Butterflies first. Chickens next. Followed by dogs and so on up to . . . (*He looks hard and long at* MORDEN.) All right (*he makes a gesture and the electronic music stops*), up, up. That's all for the time being. Now, why do you want to kill me? C'mon. I don't have all day. Why *do* you want to kill me?

MORDEN: Oh . . because . . . huh? . . . Debden . . . I remember . . . You did something to Debden.

FATHER ONGAR: What?

MORDEN: I don't know.

FATHER ONGAR: I did what you don't know? That doesn't quite make sense, Mord.

MORDEN: My name is Morden.

FATHER ONGAR: You keep insisting on that. Far be it from me to tell you who you are. But I prefer Mord. For one thing you look more like a Mord. For another, Mord rhymes with Lord and that's nice.

MORDEN: I don't know what you did. But I know the results. Debden ran out. (*He looks into the shadows.*)

FATHER ONGAR: In fact, Morden doesn't rhyme with anything much, does it? On the other hand, it is better than Merde, say. You wouldn't want to be called Mr. Merde, eh, Mr. Morden? (*He makes a gesture and the electronic music comes up.*) What's the matter?

MORDEN: That music . . .

FATHER ONGAR: Like it, eh? I'm using it next Sunday. The first electronic Mass. Hereabouts, anyway. The jazz, the modern dance, the happenings . . . all passé. I think this should goose the congregation, don't you? Although I really wonder. I sometimes think that even if Christ himself came down the aisles, frugging—wearing naught but a jock strap—or naught itself . . . Where are you going, Mord?

MORDEN: To look in there.

FATHER ONGAR: Don't.

MORDEN: Why?

FATHER ONGAR: Because I keep my harem of nude altar boys in there.

MORDEN: Is Debden there?

FATHER ONGAR: No.

MORDEN: I don't believe you.

FATHER ONGAR: What? You don't believe your priest?

MORDEN: You're not my priest.

FATHER ONGAR: What? Speak up! I can't hear you, Mord.

MORDEN: YOU'RE NOT MY PRIEST!

FATHER ONGAR: Stop, I said! Don't go in there. (*Pause.*) Not your priest? If you say so. Perhaps I'm not a priest at all. Perhaps I'm Beelzebub disguised as a caretaker who, at the moment, is disguised as a priest in order to —what? Be your tormentor? (*Laughs.*) Of course I'm your priest. If not me, who then? Father Uxbridge?

MORDEN: No. He used me.

FATHER ONGAR: Of course: He's desperately trying to find his place in today's clerical scheme of things. He won't make it, of course. Too much tradition in the blood. No natural instinct for the contemporary. However, it was shocking—that vicious rumor started against old Ux. You know, the celibacy article. Oh, Morden, there's cruelty afoot all over the thin crust of God's earth. (*Quick change of tone.*) So, he used you. Well, aren't you using me? For your inadequacies with Debden?

MORDEN: What?

FATHER ONGAR: Do you use God this way, Morden?

MORDEN: What are you talking about?

FATHER ONGAR: Do you blame Him for your situation in life? I'll bet you do. Free will, Morden. You heard of free will, haven't you? That means you're a free agent; free to choose right from wrong, good from evil. Oh, it is quite true that it doesn't matter in the long run—that your finger prints are frozen right from the start, no matter what. Still, one can still move one's fingers and point one's hand in a variety of directions. N'est ce pas, Mord?

MORDEN: I don't know what you're talking about. And don't call me Mord. I've had enough of your sermons and wise talk. I'm not here for that. And CAN'T YOU TURN THAT MUSIC OFF?

FATHER ONGAR *makes a gesture and the electronic music stops.*

FATHER ONGAR: You have no sense of humor. *And* you certainly have no musical taste. And you're not going in there.

MORDEN: Get out of my way.

FATHER ONGAR: No.
MORDEN: I'm prepared to kill you.

FATHER ONGAR *takes Morden's hands and places them around his, Ongar's own throat. Pause.*

MORDEN: I can't do it. Priests represent God Himself. I was brought up to believe that.
FATHER ONGAR: Morden, Morden, listen to me. Forget your microscopic problems. Go on out and get yourself involved. Find yourself an issue. Something you can be against. It doesn't matter what. You don't even have to feel it deeply. Just find it. Finding it is all that matters. There's got to be something. Vietnam? . . . Civil rights? . . . Crime in the streets? . . . Air pollution? . . . Low wages? . . . Too high wages? . . . Inadequate garbage collection? . . . Inadequate garbage? Ah—corruption and extortion . . . graft, Morden, Graft! . . . The bomb. The rape of the land. The traffic in the sky. High cost of living. Higher cost of dying—of education—of *truffles*. There are fights, Morden. Enough to occupy a man for two lifetimes . . . Consider . . .
MORDEN: No. I don't want to consider . . .
FATHER ONGAR: . . . the curse of canker sores.
MORDEN: . . . any of this . . .
FATHER ONGAR: Cancer and hemorrhoids.
MORDEN: . . . anymore.
FATHER ONGAR. The rise of troilism—and sodomy—not to mention coprologia.
MORDEN: Will you stop!
FATHER ONGAR: The inundation of noise.
MORDEN: Please . . .
FATHER ONGAR: The inhalation of cigarettes. Pot. Bus exhaust.
MORDEN: Please . . . please leave me alone.
FATHER ONGAR: Emphysema, Morden. Muscular dystrophy, Morden.
MORDEN: I'm here for something else.

FATHER ONGAR: Cystic fibrosis, Morden. Mental psychosis, Morden.

MORDEN: Stop it. (*He continues saying "stop, stop, stop."*)

FATHER ONGAR: Materialistic dehumanization, Morden. Opulence. Influence. Affluence. Wife swapping, Morden . . . not to mention the heartless practice of clerical chastity.

The choir of angels sings one chord.

MORDEN: There! There! That's what you really are. Not a priest. You're the anti-Christ and a fornicator.

FATHER ONGAR: I am not a fornicator.

MORDEN: Oh, yes, that's what it's all about. All this . . . all you want is to (*lowers voice*) screw.

FATHER ONGAR: What? Speak up!

MORDEN: SCREW! It's disgusting. (*Pause.*) All my life I've been miserable. All right. If my cross *was* to be miserable, I could at least look over at the Church and feel better when I saw my priest was carrying the cross of celibacy. For me. That's right. Being pure. Suffering. For me . . . FOR ME! What'll I have if you can screw too? You have already, for all I know, with my Debden.

FATHER ONGAR: Others may have, Morden. But not I.

MORDEN: Who? What others?

FATHER ONGAR: Forget her, Morden. She was unfulfilled with you. She had this great sense of loss, Morden. Loss. Do you understand loss, Morden? It was agony for her, the whole thing. She hated to hurt you, but she couldn't stand you anymore. She gave herself to . . .

MORDEN: To who? She's scarred, crippled! Who would want her?

FATHER ONGAR: There are those turned on by scars and limps. But that just disgusted her—filled her with self-loathing. She tried to kill herself. Did you know that?

MORDEN: Yes.

FATHER ONGAR: You would have had a corpse on your hands. She had to leave you. What was the alternative?

MORDEN: I don't know, Father. But you see . . . through it all . . . my whole life . . . there's at least been someone with me. I said before I was afraid of the dark. But with Debden, you see, Debden used to hold me.

FATHER ONGAR: Well, she can't anymore. And that's the reality of the situation.

MORDEN: Maybe if I talk to her.

FATHER ONGAR: You already have.

MORDEN: I mean with someone else around.

FATHER ONGAR: Me?

MORDEN: Yes.

FATHER ONGAR: Waste of time.

MORDEN: Maybe not.

FATHER ONGAR: You have nothing to offer.

MORDEN: I was good to her.

FATHER ONGAR: Goodness is irrelevant.

MORDEN: I loved the child.

FATHER ONGAR: Loving is irrelevant.

MORDEN: I'll protect them . . .

FATHER ONGAR: From whom?

MORDEN: The rest.

FATHER ONGAR: How?

MORDEN: Don't you understand? I need them.

FATHER ONGAR: Needing is irrelevant.

MORDEN: And I know they need me.

FATHER ONGAR: You are irrelevant. Now, Morden, it's time to be cruel. To make you see yourself as you really are. We are all nothing in the eyes of God. But there is an aristocracy of nothingness and you are the lowest caste of us all.

MORDEN: No. I am not nothing . . .

FATHER ONGAR: Well, *some*thing, perhaps. A cavity in the foul mouth of the world. The irritation that begins the cancer. An aborted fetus. A condom floating in the river with the rest of the garbage. A discarded prepuce. A crab in God's pubic hair. Yes, these are indeed something and you may be some or all of them, but I don't care. I'm putting a close to all this. Goodbye, Morden. You've served your purpose; helped me with my sermon. Now, if you'd care to continue demonstrating for me at some future date—fine. You'll have to be completely naked, of course. And at some point we'll get beyond just acting and you'll have to actually suffer. Maybe we'll do a Saint Sebastian. Have the congregation shoot arrows into you —Morden, where are you?

MORDEN: Here.

FATHER ONGAR: Morden?

MORDEN: Right here.

FATHER ONGAR: Why, he's left! Perhaps that's best.

MORDEN: I haven't left and you know it.

FATHER ONGAR: He might have kept trying to see what was in the other room.

MORDEN: I will see what's in there.

From now until the end of the scene, MORDEN *tries to get past* FATHER ONGAR, *who never lets him.*

FATHER ONGAR: He was frightened of the abyss in the dark in his own room . . .

MORDEN: I know Debden is in there . . .

FATHER ONGAR: . . . imagine his fright if he were to actually get into that room; see *that* abyss . . .

MORDEN: Let me pass. Let me pass. She'll listen if she sees me.

FATHER ONGAR: Well, to get back to work. I'll finish the grand sermon . . .

MORDEN: She's got to . . .

FATHER ONGAR: There's time, but not too much time . . .

MORDEN (*shouting over Father Ongar's shoulders*): Debden . . . please come back. You know what it's like to be alone.

The singer is heard singing Bach's "Seufzer, Tranen, Kummer, Not."

FATHER ONGAR (*pummeling* MORDEN, *who sinks to his knees*): Damn! Damn! Damn! They're rehearsing that damned Bach. All right. If I can't annihilate Bach yet, I can at least drown him out.

He makes a gesture. The electronic music comes up very loud for a short while. FATHER ONGAR *turns and disappears. The electronic music stops. The singer continues singing softly throughout the remainder of the play. A low hum, which will crescendo, is also heard.*

MORDEN: Alone. (*Listens.*) Wait . . . wait . . . Oh, yes . . . (*He runs to the elevator and resumes his position holding down trap to keep* FATHER ONGAR *from climbing down.* MRS. BETHNAL-GREEN *is on the floor, weaker than ever.*) Hear that hum, Father Ongar?

FATHER ONGAR: I'm coming down, Morden!

MRS. BETHNAL-GREEN (*weakly*): Yes. Help. Help.

MORDEN: That's the motor revving up, Father Ongar. Maybe it's going to start. And you know what *that* means. That means it may go up and crush you against the roof. Or it may fall and leave you hanging from the cable.

FATHER ONGAR: I'm coming down, Morden.

MORDEN: Then again, if that hum hits a certain pitch . . . a certain loud, high pitch that I'm familiar with . . . (*hum begins to ascend the scale and crescendo*) . . . then it may start going crazy. Start fast. Stop suddenly. Then start, up, up. The last time it happened, I pushed the stop button and it stopped. But if I let it go . . .

MRS. BETHNAL-GREEN *begins praying.*

FATHER ONGAR: All right, Morden . . .

MORDEN: It's Mord, Father. Remember? Rhymes with Lord.

FATHER ONGAR: I'm at the trap door. Please let go.

MORDEN: Ooooooooooooooh, it's approaching that pitch all right. God, the piper . . . Sounds like a violin. Hear it? (*The sound does, in fact, become a violin playing a sustained high note.* MORDEN *hums the note.*) Lovely. I wish

I could identify it. I have a good ear, always did. I could have been a tuner, I'll bet, but they never gave me lessons.

FATHER ONGAR: Morden!

MORDEN: There it is. There's the pitch. Now I'll smash on right through the roof. (*He sings the pitch as loud as he can.*)

A loud snapping sound and a twang. MORDEN *is thrown against the rear wall and* MRS. BETHNAL-GREEN *rolls along the floor against the wall.* FATHER ONGAR *falls into the elevator. They're all thrown against the other wall.* MRS. BETHNAL-GREEN *screams.*

FATHER ONGAR: The stop button . . . (*He lunges for it.*)

MORDEN: No.

He tries to stop FATHER ONGAR *from reaching the stop button. They're thrown against another wall. Then* MORDEN *moves in front, blocking the buttons.*

FATHER ONGAR: Yes. (*He flings himself toward* MORDEN, *yanks him aside, and pushes a button. The sound of screeching and grinding and little explosions. The three in the elevator move and shake as if the elevator were shuddering. The lights go out briefly and come up fast.* MRS. BETHNAL-GREEN *is moaning.* FATHER ONGAR *is standing over* MORDEN, *who is knocked out on the floor.*) Morden!

MORDEN (*coming around very slowly*): Did . . . I . . . smash . . . through? . . .

MORDEN *opens his eyes and looks out over the audience. The singer finishes singing as the lights fade out.*

Muzeeka

John Guare

JOHN GUARE

Muzeeka is another Obie Award-winning play to come out of the Waterford Conference, 1967. It introduces the inventive, unpredictable imagination of John Guare, whose satire not only finds a special language for laughter but a distinct, unique voice. There is nothing ambiguous in Guare's view of the world. A merry-andrew in a mechanized universe, a wise guy who defends himself against organized absurdity with the armor of raillery, *Muzeeka* has the energy, polish, and fey surprise which stamp Guare as a genuine stage satirist. He has the capacity for disgust which is an important asset to men of his calling, but he also cares about his audience, coaxing them into laughter and then using it against them. His play is difficult, often wildly funny, and, if the wind is right, devastating to all opponents.

The play is a fantasy about Jack Argue (that's an anagram for Guare)—a dreamer: soft, failing, betrayed into a tepid middle-class life. The terrain may be familiar, but Guare stamps it with its own bravura sense of fun—songs, subliminal announcements, voice-overs. Argue opens the play singing a penny, spends a night of underground sex getting a Chinese basket job, and ends his retreat from the clutches of national vapidity by fighting in Vietnam under special contract to CBS. Guare's disgust raises the real to the outrageous, but always focuses on the outlandishness of a technical society which distorts war as it does life.

Guare's humor is a mixture of a flamboyant, relaxed sense of language and a flair for gesture which can approach the cynical horror of a Grosz cartoon. In the brothel, the whore (played with side-splitting deadpan by Peggy Pope, who originated the role in Waterford) takes off her pink stockings, assuming the romantic tones of an Edith Piaf resistance pose. Her stocking, slowly rolled down her leg, is suddenly transformed into the image of a prophylactic. The effect is brilliant, and delightfully crude. The whore returns at the end of the play in a cruelly acerbic takeoff on the Martha Raye mentality—singing a song which skewers the heroes who are born anew with each headline. Dressed in an army jump suit, she strips to a bikini made of torn copies of newspapers, singing as she reads each temporary name:

> Bonnie and Clyde
> & Jesus Christ
> Rocky and Romney
> & Jesus Christ
> Johnny Carson
> & Jesus Christ
> Television
> & Jesus Christ
> Eugene McCarthy
> May be Jesus Christ

Guare, at 30, has developed his special comic language. Languorous and erotic, it creates a very special poetry as well as laughter. Argue, employed by the Muzeeka Corporation of America muses about the Etruscans, and then on how he plans to change the world. The speech is more than a dramatic ploy: it is a satirist's aesthetic—a plan for change:

> I'll start first with the violins. The Old Give 'Em What They Want. I'll wait with my tongue in my cheek here like a private smirking soul kiss and when I'm piped into every elevator, every office, every escalator, every toilet, every airplane, bus, truck and car in this country, I'll strike . . . I'll wait till all humans are inured to the everpresent inescapable background ocean blandness of my music, till everyone knows down deep I'll always be there, stroking the cortical overlay till it's hard and brittle as the clay of an Etruscan pot and then on a sudden day that is not especially spring, not especially summer, a day when the most exciting thing around is the new issue of the Reader's Digest, and you read with interest an ad that says Campbell is putting out a new flavor soup, I'll strike. That kind of day. I'll pipe in my own secret music that I keep hidden under my cortical overlay and I'll free all the Etruscans in all our brains. . . . and the country will remember its Etruscan forebears and begin dancing. . . .

Guare's capacity for joy, his love of life as well as his rage, make him at once appealing and complicated. But *Muzeeka* shows a playwright taking big risks on stage, and with them come glossy, new possibilities for the theater. The effects of Guare's boldness will only be read in his future work, but in steering his craft into the headwind of contemporary life with fresh language and vigorous form, he encounters something ambiguous and thrilling in American life.

Muzeeka was given its first New York performance at the Provincetown Playhouse, on April 28, 1968. It was directed by Melvin Bernhardt and designed by Peter Harvey, and produced by Betty Ann Besch and Warren Lyons. The sound was by James Reichert and the lighting by Johnny Dodd. The stage movement was by Ralf Harmer. The cast was as follows:

JACK ARGUE	Burt Brinckerhoff
HIS WIFE	Marcia Jean Kurtz
EVELYN LANDIS	Peggy Pope
NUMBER TWO	Sandy Baron
STAGEHANDS	Kevin Brian Conway, John Lawlor, Frank Prendergast

Prior to the New York production, the play was first performed at the Eugene O'Neill Memorial Theatre Foundation in Waterford, Connecticut.

CHARACTERS

JACK ARGUE

HIS WIFE

EVELYN LANDIS

NUMBER TWO

Three or Four STAGEHANDS

The play is in six scenes.

The time is from 1965 to 1967.

The only piece of scenery is a double bunk bed.

I Scene One

The STAGEHANDS *carry across an enormous banner, as they will at the beginning of each scene. It reads:* "IN WHICH ARGUE SINGS THE PENNY." ARGUE *is sitting on the edge of the lower bunk.*

ARGUE (*sings*):

United States of America
E Pluribus Unum
O
N
E
(*Speaks:*) Cent (*Turns coin over. Sings:*)
In God We Trust
L
I
B
Eeeeeee
R
Teeeeee
Y
(*Speaks:*) 1965.
Flips coin.
He makes a choice.
Uncovers coin.
He stands up, beaming.

ARGUE: Heads!

Blackout

Scene Two

"IN WHICH ARGUE SAYS 'I LOVE YOU.' "

ARGUE *and his* WIFE *are in the lower bunk making love. He smiles at her and touches her face.*

ARGUE: I love you.

Blackout

Argue's WIFE *is furiously turning the pages of a magazine.*

ARGUE (*desperate*): I love you.

Blackout

ARGUE *sits up reading* Playboy *magazine. His* WIFE *is sobbing.*

ARGUE (*blandly*): I love you.

Blackout

Scene Three

"IN WHICH ARGUE HAS A VISION."

ARGUE *sits on the edge of the lower bunk. His* WIFE, *lying in the lower bunk covered by a sheet, watches him, one arm over her head, one eye showing, watching.*

ARGUE: If I could've been born anybody—my pick of a Kennedy or a Frank Sinatra or a Ford or the King of Greece—out of that whole hat of births, I still would've picked to be an Etruscan. Nobody knows where they came from. The archaeologists guess maybe they were one of the first tribes of Rome about a million years ago when Romulus and Remus were posing for that Roman statue—that baby picture—of them suckling life from a wolf. Well, Romulus and Uncle Remus must've hoarded all that wolf milk to themselves because the Etruscans vanished without a trace, like a high, curved wave that breaks on the sand and retreats right back into the sea. Vanished. Poof. Splash.

And the only footprints the Etruscans left behind were these jugs. These jugs and pots and bottles and urns covered with pictures. Line drawings much like Picasso's. The whole world can sue me for libel but I accuse Pablo Picasso of stealing all his line drawings from the Etruscans. J'accuse! J'accuse Pablo Picasso! Pots and jugs covered with people dancing. ALL dancing. Warriors

dancing. Men dancing. Women dancing. Servants dancing. Prostitutes dancing. Old men with bottles of wine and they're dancing. A whole civilization dancing. Every part of them dancing. Not just their feet, but their hands and heads and beards and peckers and bosoms and shoulders and noses and toes all dancing. And these smiles—these lovely, loony smiles—that should make them look like a race of Alfred E. Newmans except only genius could know the joy that's painted on those pots and bottles and urns. All painted in earth colors: blacks and browns and tans and white. A whole civilization danced up out of the earth. Danced up out of the ground all over the ground and vanished. Maybe they just danced right into the pots and what we see being held prisoner in museums is not line drawings of Etruscans, but the Etruscans themselves, dancing right inside the pots. If I could've been born anybody in the world ever —a Kennedy or Sinatra or Henry Ford or the King of Greece—I still would've picked out of that whole hat of births, picked Etruscan.
I'm going to take the job with Muzeeka, Sally-Jane.

He stands up and pulls on trousers and slips an already tied necktie over his head.

Three STAGEHANDS *come forward. 1 assumes a chair-like position. 2 sits on him as the Boss. 3 kneels on all fours.* ARGUE *sits on him.*

ARGUE (*earnestly, suavely, to the Boss*): I can't compose, but I can arrange and, Sir, I want to be with the biggest largest piped-in music company in the whole wide world, so I'm picking the Muzeeka Corporation of America International over all the record companies and movie studios I've had offers from. (*The Boss thinks a very long moment.* ARGUE *leans forward in suspense. The Boss stands up, beaming. He shakes hands with* ARGUE.

ARGUE *pumps his hand with both hands and turns to us.*) I'm in! I'm in!

Muzak plays, blandly. The three STAGEHANDS *sit cross-legged in a row and pantomime playing violins and horns.* ARGUE *conducts them but talks over his shoulder to us.*

ARGUE (*to us*): I'll start first with the violins. The Old Give 'Em What They Want. I'll wait with my tongue in my cheek here like a private smirking soul-kiss and when I'm piped into every elevator, every office, every escalator, every toilet, every home, airplane, bus, truck and car in this country, I'll strike. (*The* STAGEHANDS *fade away.* ARGUE *turns full to us.*) Do you know about the cortical overlay that covers fifty percent of the human brain, deadening all our instincts so we have to be given lessons in every facet of living—except dying, of course. The human and the dolphin are the only animals that have this clay pot on the brain. How the dolphins manage to survive, I can't figure out. But they'll have to take care of themselves. I'm involved with the humans.
I'll wait till all humans are inured to the everpresent, inescapable background ocean blandness of my music, till everyone knows down deep I'll always be there, stroking that cortical overlay till it's as hard and brittle as the clay of an Etruscan pot and then, on a sudden day that is not especially spring, not especially summer, a day when the most exciting thing around is the new issue of the *Reader's Digest,* and you read with interest an ad that says Campbell just invented a new-flavor soup, I'll strike. That kind of a day. I'll pipe in my own secret music that I keep hidden here under my cortical overlay and I'll free all the Etruscans in all our brains. Not rock and roll. No, more than that. A blend of Rock and Mozart and Wagnerian Liebestods and Gregorian chants. Eskimo folk songs. African. Greek. Hindoo. All

bound together by drums that will fascistically force its *way* through the over*lay* and the country will remember its Etruscan forebears and begin dancing.
I'll sit in my office turning the level of volume louder and louder and watch the fires in the distance as men throw in their attaché cases, their Buicks, their split-level homes and mortgages and commuter tickets and railroad trains and husbands and wives and children and bosses and enemies and friends.
On planes, pilots will race to the sea and passengers will slug the smiles off stewardesses and stewardesses will pour hot coffee on all the regular passengers. Bald people—hairless men, hairless ladies—will whip off their wigs and eyebrows and grease their skulls and bodies with black car-grease so the moon will reflect on them when they dance.
Everybody will feel sexy all the time and nobody will mind what anybody does to anybody else and twins in wombs will dance so that girl babies will be born with babies within them and those babies will have babies within them and within them and within and within.
Buses gallop down Fifth Avenue crammed with naked people beeping the horn, riding on the sidewalk, looting all the stores, making love in all the churches, knocking noses off plaster saints and never getting out of the bus. They drive the bus down to a subway full of naked dancing people eating pictures of Chinese food off the posters in the subway and the train pulls in and all the naked people push the train off the tracks and leap onto the third rail to see what electricity tastes like. They race up to Harlem where naked Negroes have flooded the streets with fat and are chicken-frying Puerto Ricans who cha cha cha and everybody's skin blisters and crackles in cha-cha time. The Negroes skewer white people onto maracas and we all dance and devour each other and belch and nobody dies because we've forgotten to and our rib cages become bars of

music and our eyes and ears behind the rib cages are notes of music and our spines are staff notes holding us up high and everyone's body is a dance floor and the dancing sets our planet loose and we'll tumble around in galaxies *until,*
in exhaustion, the world will settle back into place and rest and rest and we shall have the beautiful peace of exhaustion.
For that is all peace is—isn't it—exhaustion? The peace of sadness. After copulation all men are sad? And the peace will be sad and slow of breath and even a vague disgust . . .
but there will be exhaustion and yes a contentment and, yes, there shall be peace . . .
I'm going to take the job with Muzeeka, Sally-Jane.

He jumps joyously back in bed with his WIFE.

Blackout

Scene Four

Two STAGEHANDS *enter carrying banner that reads:* "IN WHICH ARGUE MAKES A TERRIBLE DISCOVERY ABOUT HIMSELF."

A blowzy blonde in bed in the lower bunk. Sleepy, drugged. One gorgeous leg hangs over the edge of the bed.

A STAGEHAND *appears at the rear of the stage carrying a brightly painted door.* ARGUE *follows after it. His raincoat and hat are soaking wet. He is nervous, excited, hesitant. He knocks against the door, upstage right.*

ARGUE (*a whisper*): Evelyn Landis? (*No response. The door moves up left. He knocks.*) Miss Evelyn Landis? (*No response. The door moves down left. He knocks.*) Evelyn Landis? (*No response. She stirs. The door moves down center. He knocks.*) Miss Evelyn Landis?

EVELYN LANDIS (*fearful; sudden*): Yes? (*She sits up, groggy.*)

ARGUE: Miss Evelyn Landis?

EVELYN LANDIS (*afraid*): Who is it?

ARGUE: Miss Evelyn Landis?

EVELYN LANDIS (*getting up*): Western Union?

ARGUE: Ahhhh, you're in—

She is at the door. She bends down, her hand extended.

EVELYN LANDIS: Slip it under the door.

ARGUE (*pause; nervous laughter*): That'd be a trick—a feat of some doing—(*She opens the door a crack. She peeks out. He peeks in.*) I couldn't—ha—slip it under the door. A lovely night out. Hello. Let me dribble off. (*He takes his hat off. The water catches her. She holds her foot against the door so he can't get in.*) It's been raining. Right through to the bone. Have you seen the streets? The colors the neon put in the streets? I thought blood had been spilled in the streets—a massacre all the way up Sixth Avenue. But it's only the traffic lights and when they change the blood turns to green—verdant—green—then the lights burst into these geraniums and the streets have blood again and then green again. Springlike. (*Her ear is pressed against the door trying to figure out who the hell this is.*) I saw your ad. In a men's room in a bar on Greenwich . . . I flushed and saw your name and flushed and blushed, but returned and saw your name and this address and what you did spelled out in a neat, very sincere hand. My wife, Sally-Jane, knows something about handwriting and I've picked up some analysis from her, and we cross our T's —not my wife and I but you and I cross our T's in a way that spells out bizarreness of desire, but a sincerity behind that bizarre . . . it's all there in your T's—in the angle of them over the urinal . . . (*Suddenly embarrassed.*) I hope it's not a joke. Some friend or enemy playing tricks. It's a vicious trick if it's a joke and you should send someone in there with Ivory soap and water and scrub, scrub it if it's a trick.

She signals to a STAGEHAND *who enters with a large piece of poster board and a pen. She draws an enormous "T" on the board. It looks like a child's "T," a Palmer Method "T." She hands* ARGUE *the board through the narrow crack of the door. He looks at it.*

ARGUE: That's the "T"! (*The* STAGEHAND *takes the board and exits.*) Yes, I knew there was no joke in your name. Evelyn Landis. Your address. Your phone number. And I was walking thinking of you and what the ad said you did—the graffiti said you did—and watching the traffic lights change the streets from blood to grass and then to blood and then to grass and then I found myself—small miracle—here by your address and a bell by your name. A golden bell with many finger indentations on it . . . (*hesitation*) . . . and I didn't call. I should have . . . (*strong:*) No, I didn't want to and here I am and I wonder if I could come in and you could do to me what the bathroom wall in that bar over on—(*His voice cracks high.*) Do you know the bar? Over on—I'll pay even though it said you did what you did for nothing, but no matter what Chock Full O'Nuts says, there's no law against tipping. Ha? Ha? Yes?

EVELYN LANDIS: No law against tipping.

She opens the door. The STAGEHAND *takes it away.* ARGUE *steps in, remembers to wipe his feet. Takes off his raincoat and shakes the wet off it. A* STAGEHAND *appears as a hatrack.* ARGUE *hangs the coat on it. The* STAGEHAND *exits.* ARGUE *smiles broadly at her.*

ARGUE: It's not a joke? You do do what the bathroom wall said you did?

She instantly transforms into Argue's idea of the ideal French whore. She poses on the bed and peels off her stockings.

EVELYN LANDIS: Ees eet true or not? Zee point ees some Juan said eet. SomeJuan wrote eet. Writting. We mosst trost zee written word. Eef I say Non, eet ees zee lie feelthy, you would feel zee embarrassment. I would feel zee cheepning. You would trost no words for a long time, look on zee written word wiz zee eye yellowed by (*she pulls the stocking off*) Jaundice! (*Soul weary:*) I want you to believe. I want to believe. I want what someJuan has claimed (*the other stocking off*) partout moi to be true. Eef we act out zee lies, make trooth of zee lies every-Juan say partout nous, zen we would have wage zee major victory on lies, on hate in zee world . . . (*Joan of Arc:*) When a lie becomes truth, eet ees strong. We mosst feed lies ze tiger's milk of truth and in making lies truth we celebrate truth—assassinate BangBang zee lies . . . (*Then, flatly:*) What did they say about me?

ARGUE (*extending a piece of paper*): I wrote out the whole ad—with your address.

She takes the paper and reads it a long time. She looks at him. She reads it again. She returns it.

EVELYN LANDIS (*very weary*): I better get ready . . . (*She exits.*)

He loosens his tie and takes off his shoes and socks. He looks to make sure she's gone. A STAGEHAND *enters with a telephone.* ARGUE *dials as secretly and quietly as he can. Perhaps the* STAGEHAND *makes dialing noises, then ringing noises.* ARGUE *hushes him.*

ARGUE (*into the phone*): Maternity ward, please . . . Sixth floor, please . . . (*Urgently:*) This is Mr. Argue. Jack. How is she? . . . Oh God oh God. Is she waiting till the kid is ready for college? . . . Can you look in? Take a peek inside? A boy? A girl? (*The operator is obviously shocked. Placating:*) All right, all right, if she's conscious, tell her I love her. (*Pause.*) I. L. O. V.—Y. That's right U. and sign it her husband. (*Pause.*) J. A. C. K. That's right. I am at a number where I can be reached. 470–0150. Yes, I'll be here. (EVELYN LANDIS *re-enters carrying a large round heavy flat basket with a hole in the middle of it. Three strands of long strong rope are attached to the basket's rim. The basket is decorated with spangles and streamers and swirls of day-glo colors. She plops it down onto the ground. She stares at him.* ARGUE *is embarrassed to be caught with the phone. He holds out the receiver. Laughs nervously.*) I took the liberty—my wife is in labor. (*He hangs up the phone. The* STAGEHAND *exits.*) Just a local call. St. Vincent's Hospital over on Greenwich . . . They didn't need me. She's been in labor eight hours now. They told me to take a few hours off. Nothing more useless than a father at a delivery. Ha? Even animal fathers go away and hunt till the female has cubbed or foaled or hatched or—well, except the sea horse. He does the birthing himself. (*She sets the basket down. Then he, brightly:*) I—I—I haven't been in the Village in years, since college a few years ago. Am I in Greenwich or East? Which Village is this? I saw all you people swarming the streets tonight, you revolters, you rebels with your hair and flowers and beards and birds and braids and boots and beads and I look in your eyes for the visions drugs have given you and tonight I admire you—love you so much. Your freedom. Your left-wing connections have covered you with wings and I want to become—touch some part of—fly up there with you into the Underground. (*She thinks about that for a minute.*) Oh, I have my subscription to the *Evergreen Review,* but I still seem so removed. I live in Greenwich. Not the Village, but Connecticut. Well, not Greenwich actually, but right outside—Kennedy, Connecticut—new development, but nice—and I don't get down to the Village very much and now, with the baby, I suppose I won't be getting down here—oh, maybe to see an Off-Broadway show if it gets good notices—(*No response from her.*) *The Fantasticks.* (*Pause.*) I'll have to see that sometime. (*Pause.*) I suppose it'll be around forever.

EVELYN LANDIS: You don't have to make a good impression on me. (*She moves to the bed with the basket.*)

ARGUE (*leaning against the post of the bed*): I'm sorry . . . I want to connect in some way. Tonight I've been remembering a vision you could call it I had on my honeymoon a few years ago. I was twenty-two. I'm twenty-eight now, but I could be thirty-eight or forty-eight or a hundred and eight—and tonight my wife in pain—Sally-Jane in pain—not needing me. Feeling violent yes walking down here pressing close to you all, feeling my own labor pains, my own dreams locked in by this cortical overlay and maybe my pains are no more than sympathy pains, but that gives them no less reality, you know? And you see. I had plans. (*Muzak plays. A* STAGEHAND *enters right with a sign*): "HE HAD PLANS." (*A* STAGEHAND *enters left with another sign*): "WITH HIS MUSIC." (*The first* STAGEHAND *turns his sign over. It says*): "BUT ALL HE PLANNED." (*The second* STAGEHAND *turns his sign over. It says*): "TURNED BLAND." Bland . . . tonight my cortical overlay weighs down on me and tonight in that bar I saw your words—well, they're not exactly Mene Mene Tekel—but my home state gave me my clue. Connecticut. I want to connect. Therefore, I must cut. Cut off all the ties just for a while, so I can get back to what I was, am, am down deep. Establish my relation to all the Etruscans, all the animals. Except the dolphin, of course. Never the dolphin. Connecticut. Good Christ. Connect? I cut.

EVELYN LANDIS: Boy, are you a sickie.

ARGUE (*threatening*): I am not a sickie. I have not come here for sick reasons.

EVELYN LANDIS (*pause*): I don't want you beating me up.

ARGUE: I am here for political reasons.

EVELYN LANDIS: I just got the bandages taken off from a guy last week—

ARGUE (*cutting her off*): Look, the country is ultimately controlled by the moderates. Right? We therefore need a strong Left as well as a strong Right. Right? Two banks of a river—the Right and the Left—right?—and the river between is the river of moderation that keeps democracy flowing along. Right? I am in that river, but am no part of it and as a consequence am drowning. Right? I want to align myself with you on the Left bank. The Underground. The Left. Right? I can't be a moderate. I don't know enough about either side. But the Right is repulsive to me. I want to stop the war. I love Civil Rights. That leaves only the Left. That's all that's left. Don't you see I'm right? (*He turns to us.*) I can't go back to Connecticut a husband, a father and that's all. I have to become a citizen. I read *The New York Times* and there's a wall of clay between what's happening in the world and me. Breakthrough. That's all.

EVELYN LANDIS: You want to get this Pledge of Allegiance started?

The STAGEHANDS *enter and help her into the basket and attach it to a hook on the bottom of the upper bunk. On a signal from* EVELYN, ARGUE *gets into the bunk under the basket. When he is in place, she turns a switch, a gong sounds. Psychedelic lights go on. The* STAGEHAND *behind* EVELYN *spins her. Argue's body pumps slowly.*

EVELYN LANDIS (*to us*) : Look at this phony. He wants some wild psychedelic experience to carry in the wallet of his heart as a secret joy until he's forty when I'll have faded away and he'll have to find another me—maybe a Negress the next time—to get him through till he's fifty or sixty. Some memory to pull out of the wallet of his heart to show in the locker room of his country club, the Yale Club, the club car on the New Haven Railroad so he can feel a regular guy. And he thinks he's having some mystical experience. I'm above him. I can look down into the depths of his fantasy like a witch who reads fortunes in pools of water. He wants his mind to be a Hiroshima of lurid fantasies! Look down! Look down! His skull is a teacup—and the tea leaves of his brain spell out—

ARGUE (*in ecstasies; his body pumping up and down*) : It's a nice house. Up to my ass in mortgage. A lawn green as money. At night, a smell of pines. Really. So fresh. Chill. Mist.

EVELYN LANDIS (*to one of the* STAGEHANDS) : Could you read us his fantasy? You can't understand one word he's saying.

THE STAGEHAND (*comes downstage to us and reads to us in a flat voice*) : A nice house. Up to my ass in mortgage. A lawn green as money. At night, a smell of pines. Really. Chill. Mist. So fresh. Only thirty-five miles out of New York where my job is. You could be up in the Maine woods or it could be a hundred years ago and I'm a pioneer and the trees are big and the house is big and I feel ownership and I stand in the dark under the trees looking at the frame of yellow light in the darkness —the kitchen light I've left on that frames a portrait of what I am now and always shall be. Sally-Jane calls from the darkness of the bedroom above. "Come up, Come up" and the air is sweet and chill and I go up in the darkness knowing my way up the stairs even though we have lived here only a few months and Sally-Jane is there in bed in a negligee I bought her at Saks to make her look sexy and in this light she is sexy and in the morning the negligee is folded neatly on the needlepoint chair her aunt gave us for a wedding present and we've become one person with many arms and legs and there is the new child folded neatly within her womb and the sun nuzzles our necks like a cat that's been born during the night and I'm up to my ass in debts and I'm still half asleep, yet I smile and say "Yes, I've done the right thing . . . I love you, Sally-Jane."

One of the other STAGEHANDS *pushes an electric phone ring. It rings and rings.*

ARGUE (*moaning*) : Yes. Yes. I've done the right thing. Yes. Yes. (*Another* STAGEHAND *picks up the phone and hands it to* ARGUE.) Yes. Yes. (*Into the phone:*) This is he. He. He. Has she? It's here? It's here? It's here? It's here? It's here? (*He shudders. His body relaxes. The basket stops spinning slowly.*) I'll be right—yes—over. Yes, right over . . . (*He hangs up the phone. He is exhausted. He smiles up at her.*) I'm a father. I—I'd better go . . . (*He stands up tentatively. He wobbles and smiles. He smooths his hair back. He adjusts his tie. He takes out his wallet. He smiles truly for the first time.*) I'm a father. (*She holds out her hand. He gives her money.*) You know what I'm going to do? Knock my wife up again. Her being in St. Vincent's Hospital is the only chance I'll get to come back to the Village and I'll look you up.

EVELYN LANDIS (*taking the money*) : You phony.

ARGUE (*putting on his shoes*) : No! I'm involved. I have a share of today. I can walk back, splash those colors in the street, pick up my child and say—I don't even know what it is—I forgot to ask—but it's a child and it's alive and I can pick up my child and say "Your papa has a share of today. Your father is something. Your father dared."

EVELYN LANDIS (*like a Cheshire cat*) : You phony. You phony. You phony. You phony. You phony.

Pause.

ARGUE : Now wait a minute. That's one thing I'm—I've got friends here. (*Into the audience:*) We went to school together. We know each other from the club. We ride into New York every day. You know me. I'm no phony. I'm one of you. I've read *Catcher in the Rye*. I know what phonies are. (*He hesitates. Into the audience, a nervous laugh.*) Like Ring Lardner said, You know Me, Al? (*He looks at us.*) Don't you? Don't you? (*He smiles nervously at us and backs away offstage.*)

EVELYN LANDIS *climbs out of her basket. She sizes up audience. Bright music plays. The house lights come up full. She runs into the audience, blanketing the audience with cards that read:*

EVELYN LANDIS
133½ MacDougal Street
470–0150
Chinese Basket Job
You like?

EVELYN LANDIS (*in the audience; ad lib*):
Hello, Scarsdale!
Is that your wife? My lips are sealed.
Pass the cards down—pass 'em down!
Give that to your hubby. You come along too. Got something for everybody!
Hey! There's the bum that gave me the bandages.
(*She hurls piles of cards out. She sings:*)
Though April showers
May come your way!

She exits at the back of the house.

House lights down

Scene Five

As soon as EVELYN LANDIS *exits at the rear of the house,* ARGUE *comes downstage.*

He starts to talk to us.

His mood is charming and determinedly casual and very embarrassed.

He laughs.

He can't speak.

He smiles.

No words will come out.

He tries to speak.

Two STAGEHANDS *walk behind him with a banner that reads:* SCENE FIVE: "IN WHICH ARGUE IS AT A LOSS." *They throw it over his head.*

Blackout

Scene Six

"IN WHICH ARGUE GOES TO WAR."

Indian music plays. Ravi Shankar music.

ARGUE *is dressed in army fatigues. He sits cross-legged in front of the lower bunk and smiles at us. Calmly. Serenely. He might even keep polishing the same spot on his boot over and over again.*

The music stops.

NUMBER TWO *runs in, out of breath. He is approximately Argue's age and dressed in green fatigues and helmet and is as thick as* ARGUE *is thin. He is as desperate as* ARGUE *is calm.*

NUMBER TWO: Buddy, you got to help me. I been in binds in my life, but, buddy, you're a college man, aren't you? I figure you are—you talk with a nice way and you don't wear any school rings, so it must've been a good school. Guys say they're college men and you look at their ring and it says North Star College in Wyoming or something, but you never say nothing and you talk real nice and you are a college man and I'm in a bind.

ARGUE (*smiling*): I went to Yale and Harvard and Princeton.

NUMBER TWO: Christ. I'm nothin'—Hollywood High—a dropout—

An explosion outside. A STAGEHAND *comes downstage and bangs two garbage-can lids together.* NUMBER TWO *falls down in fright and huddles close to* ARGUE.

NUMBER TWO: Buddy, you got to help me.

ARGUE (*amazed*) : It sounds so funny to hear my schools out here. Out in a jungle. It doesn't mean anything. It suddenly—no, not suddenly, the last four months, nothing I ever learned means anything . . . (*He turns to* NUMBER TWO *for the first time. Smiles peacefully.*) I don't think I can help you.

NUMBER TWO (*whispering harshly*) : What—are you turning snob on a buddy? College guy. You think you're something. We're all in this together. Buddies are to help. Didn't you ever go swimming? The Buddy System. Well, I am holding up my hand because I am drowning.

ARGUE (*pleased*) : Ahhhhhhhhhh—

NUMBER TWO (*crawling downstage*) : Look out there. Look who's covering the battle tomorrow.

ARGUE: I saw the cameras.

NUMBER TWO: CBS.

ARGUE: I watched the Vietnamese children help drape the cameras in camouflage.

NUMBER TWO: CBS.

ARGUE: Watch them greasing the wheels so the cameras can glide down hills alongside us.

NUMBER TWO: That's it. CBS is covering the battle. I got transferred to this unit two weeks ago when my outfit got wiped out at the Mekong Delta. (*He falls on his back in despair.*) My whole unit was under exclusive contract to NBC. I'm only allowed to fight for NBC. If they see me tomorrow—CBS—they can strip me of all my rank. Cut my payments off back home. They can send me to a unit. (*He sits up.*) Christ, an independent unit. An educational network unit. I'm not fighting for no

Channel Thirteen. I don't want to break contracts. I want to kill these VC, but I can't fight tomorrow. You got to help me. You're a college man. Yale, Harvard, Princeton. Christ, you must be about eighty-six years old.

ARGUE: Yes. Yes. Twenty-six. Twenty-six!

NUMBER TWO: What the hell were you doing there?

ARGUE (*a frozen smile, reciting*): Princeton to college. Then the Yale School of Music. Then I felt I didn't know anything practical. So off to Harvard Business for a year to learn the rules of the game so I could fit in. I couldn't fit in. I got married. I worked for a year for the Muzeeka Corporation of America. I am drafted. I am happy I am drafted. I looked at my wife and child in Connecticut and thanked Uncle Sam for getting me out of the country, for escaping without the drag of becoming a missing person. I've killed many people in the four months I've been here. I've finally broken through the clay pot that covers my brain. I dance and sing while I shoot and kill. I thank God for war. War is God's invention to make us remember we are animals. Everything is out of my hands . . . I am a little Moses placed in a basket waiting in the bulrushes for my Pharaoh's daughter. I am so happy. Don't you see? Don't you see? Help you? How can I help you? How? How? (*He tries to climb into the upper bunk.*)

NUMBER TWO *grabs him up and pulls him into the lower bunk.*

NUMBER TWO: Buddy, calm down. Calm down. Look, lay down. In the bunk. Rest. Rest. You want television on? I'll put it on quiet so the VC don't hear. My old unit wasn't wiped out till the end of *Batman* and the *Ed Sullivan Show.* They must've sat in the black watching for us, watching the television till the show ended and we turned it off. I never knew whether they killed us 'cause we were the enemy or because we turned off Ed

Sullivan. (*He rolls a joint and gives it to* ARGUE.) Calm, come on. See, I'm a buddy to you.

ARGUE (*pause; calm*) : That's what gets me most. The TV's in the tents. We're here in the jungle and we have television. Tapes of all the Top Ten TV shows broadcast out of Saigon through the jungles—Martha Raye everywhere. I don't like it. It puts sweat in places I never sweat before. Look at my ankles. Soaking wet. Bones weren't meant to sweat, were they? My legs are dry, but my ankles—my ankles—

NUMBER TWO (*rubbing Argue's ankles*) : Come on—come on—you'll get R&R soon. Go to Hong Kong. Bangkok. Bang a little cock. Thailand. Land a little thigh. That's all you need. Rest. Recreation. Look, I'll tell you what we do. We put on our make-up for tomorrow's battle. We can sleep that much later in the morning.

ARGUE (*sits up, shakily; smiling*) : Yes I do want to fight tomorrow. I do want to be in good shape for tomorrow. Yes. Yes. Yes. Killing soothes. Oh, it soothes.

They get out their make-up kits from under the bed. They sit side by side on the lower bunk and make themselves up.

NUMBER TWO : Don't I recognize you from *Life?*

ARGUE : I was on the cover a month ago.

NUMBER TWO : You sign a contract with them?

ARGUE : No. No. I want to stay independent.

NUMBER TWO : You exclusive with CBS?

ARGUE : We had to. (*Stops. Falls back, laughing.*) The captain's mother lives on a mountain top in Utah and CBS is the only station she gets.

Pause. They make up, getting the eyes and cheeks and chin, with strong harsh lines; NUMBER TWO *green and black,* ARGUE *red and white.*

NUMBER TWO : Good thing about NBC—dull days when there's no fighting like Lunar New Year, they rerun our old skirmishes and we get residuals. I see my old buddies and I dream we're all together. Then I watch them get killed all over again and I see me carried off on a stretcher to have my operation photographed for *Saturday Evening Post.* Did you see the spread on me? I love rainy days when we fight only reruns.

ARGUE: CBS doesn't do that.

NUMBER TWO: Shitty outfit.

ARGUE *is calmed. He looks at* NUMBER TWO.

ARGUE: Hey, don't make yourself up so well. Do a sloppy job. They know you're new in this outfit and tell them you don't know how to make up for camera yet and they'll stick you in the rear lines out of camera.

NUMBER TWO (*very impressed*): Why didn't I think of that? (*He smears green under his eyes.*) See what a college education does.

ARGUE: No, it doesn't. It doesn't.

NUMBER TWO (*putting black lines in his cheeks*): I been on the cover of *Look* and that spread in the *Saturday Evening Post.* I been in *The New York Times* and the *L.A. Times* and the *Daily News Sunday Coloroto.* (*He shows his face to* ARGUE.)

ARGUE: A little more greenish. They hate you looking sallow. (ARGUE *puts healthy red on his cheeks.*)

NUMBER TWO (*pause*): What do you do back in civvies?

ARGUE: Civvies? I had a job. With the Muzeeka Corporation of America. Piped-in music.

NUMBER TWO: Like my dentist office?

ARGUE: We're everywhere.

NUMBER TWO: No kidding! You arrange all those violins and everything?

ARGUE: Got a degree from Yale School of Music.

NUMBER TWO: That's fantastic that Muzeeka. It deadens the pain and everything. You must've put novocaine out of business.

ARGUE: Yes. That's why I don't think I'm going back. (*The*

sudden loud whir of a helicopter booms through the theater. ARGUE *and* NUMBER TWO *roll off the bunk behind the bunk for safety. Over the whir comes a montage of LBJ's March 31, 1968 speech being broadcast to the troops from the helicopter:*) "My fellow Americans . . . South Vietnamese govern themselves . . . De-Escalate the war . . . Have decided not to seek reelection as President of the United States . . ." (ARGUE *and* NUMBER TWO *peer up from behind the bunk.*) "Now, my good soldiers, pray after me . . . Now I lay me down to sleep . . . I pray the Lord . . ."

And the machine roars away to other jungles. NUMBER TWO *has blessed himself and started praying.* ARGUE *is kneeling by* NUMBER TWO.

ARGUE (*to us*) : So it might all be over soon.
I'll believe that when it happens.
It might all be over soon! All possibilities again.
We'll go back home: A new President. A nice President.
Life will be so nice again.

Argue's WIFE *appears in a negligee. She holds out her arms and weeps tears of joy.*

WIFE : Jack's back! Jack's back! Jack's back!

The STAGEHANDS *appear, one by one, hands extended, big wide smiles.*

STAGEHANDS : Long time no see. Long time no see.
You look wonderful.
Isn't that nice.

The moment is repeated over and over. "Jack's back—Isn't that nice—you look wonderful—long time no see—" ARGUE *swings over the bed and comes all smiling down to us as if he's at a friendly interview and answering spot questions from the audience. The voices continue behind him.*

ARGUE: The killing didn't mean anything. Of course I've killed people. I've put bullets in people's eyes. Thank you! Thank you! I've put let me think bullets in yes people's ears and I've put bullets in . . . thank you very much . . . people's noses and bullets in people's bellies and bellybuttons . . . hello there! Sure is good to be back . . . and backs! Yes, people's backs. No, I never used the flames. I never burned anybody. That's one thing. I can wrap my uneaten dinner of course in Saran Wrap—Dow Chemical? Why should it bother me? I never used the flames. Yes, I said people's backs. (*The handshaking and greetings behind* ARGUE *turn into silence and the gestures turn into stroking.* ARGUE *sits at the edge of the stage.*) And I'll go back and be convinced, the *Reader's Digest* will convince me, reassure me, and the newspapers and *TV Guide* and my Muzeeka will stick their hands in my ears and massage my brain and convince me I didn't do anything wrong. And life will be so nice. And my wounds will heal and there won't even be, you won't even see, one little scar, one little bellybutton, one little memento to show that in violence I was reborn. I'll really miss the killing.

The STAGEHANDS *and Argue's wife have faded off.* NUMBER TWO *comes down to* ARGUE.

NUMBER TWO: Hey, Argue, I got an idea. My poppa told me to keep an eye out for a smart guy, a college man, which is why I'm looking at rings all the time, and now that it looks like it's over—peace feelers—take him back home with me. Take him in as a full business partner in my poppa's new business. Fifty-fifty, buddy—right down the line. It's a wonderful town. My poppa's mayor of it all and my ma wins bright blue ribbons from miles around for her beef pot pies and we ride horses and drive cars under oranges that fall from all the palm trees because it *is* country except there's fabulous surf only fifty miles away and the sun always shines except when it's night. *Two* movie theaters. Would you want to come back? Ahhh, you wouldn't be interested. You're an Easterner. Big college man. But my poppa's new business . . . It's gonna be big, Argue. BIG.

ARGUE (*after a pause, comes down to us*) : I see what I must do. They tell us—all the sergeants and generals—that we're fighting for democracy. I've never been anywhere near democracy. I meet men from all over America and I realize my America—New York, Boston, Washington, all the towns in between—have nothing to do with America. They're—we're a suburb of Europe. I'll return to the real America, but move to the Midwest, the Far West, the Northwest. It *is* the buddy system and he has saved my life. I'll divorce Sally-Jane and move out West. Marry a girl from North Dakota. South Dakota. Either Dakota. I don't care. And work with him and forget about changing the world. Work simply. That's the answer and I won't care about Negroes or Civil Rights or Hippies or Music of the Middle East or lies or the Etruscans or anything because I'll be a member of a small town and live there and that's my whole world.

NUMBER TWO: My company is based on the Roto-Rooter. In Poli, California, where I live now, you can see my sign flashing over the whole San Juarez Valley. The sign's at the top of the San Juarez mountains in high red neon letters—not red red, more like the red in a sunset—more of a pink—my sign flashes and the red glare shines even into Los Angeles if the smog is down: *You Poop It We Scoop It.*

ARGUE: What?

NUMBER TWO: But what we're gonna do—my poppa and me and you—is to move over the whole country with our Roto-Rooter—the same cesspool principle—but hooked up to atomic power. Atomic-powered disposals. Oh, it's wonderful being in cesspools. You lift up the septic tank and look in and know what people have flushed away. Better than reading palms or handwriting analysis, you can tell a person by the secret things they flush away. If we cover cross-country with our Atomic-Powered Sooper Dooper-Pooper Scooper—yes! that's what I'll call it—yes, yes, we can take over the world, the good we can do under ghettos. My dream! Install my SooperDooper under all the places that give America a bad name, that cancel out all the good we're doing here. If there's a riot—trouble—long hot summer, oh God! We pull that chain, our atomic-powered chain and flush away Detroit, Watts, Newark. Flush them away, clean. Clean. Cool. (*He is beaming.*) And I want you in on it with me, Argue. America: one big cesspool in our hands. You're a smart man and a nice appearance and a pleasant personality and an obvious college education and my wife's got a sister and the four of us—our cesspools powered by the sun—spreading out from Los Angeles like an ink blot on an enormous United States-shaped blotter.

ARGUE (*quiet*): Is that it?

NUMBER TWO: Huh?

ARGUE: Is that all we're fighting for?

NUMBER TWO (*stretching blissfully*): That's what I'm scratching the days off my calendar for.

A STAGEHAND *crosses the stage wearing a sandwich board. It says:* "GET YOUR HEART IN AMERICA." "HEART" *is not spelled, but is a picture of a heart. When he turns, the other side says:* "OR GET YOUR ASS OUT." "ASS" *is a drawing of a donkey.*

ARGUE (*to us; rueful*): I wish I'd been born a black . . . and when I got back home, I'd loot all the houses including my own and march to TV stores and lift open the store window like a giant automat and Sally-Jane and I would watch newsreels of ourselves . . . And instead I'll go back home and do the only thing I can do, make my Muzeeka, and we'll be piped into rocket ships and rocketed from planet to planet, galaxy to galaxy and the universe will be so nice. So nice. When I go home, I am what is being looted.

NUMBER TWO (*gets into the lower bunk*) : Hey, Argue buddy, tomorrow let's get some special VC and cut off their ears and we'll get them bronzed and hang them over our desk when we get back Stateside.

ARGUE (*sitting on the edge of the upper bunk*) : Yes. Sure. Good idea. Yes. (*He reaches to the rear bedpost and takes a machete from it.*)

NUMBER TWO: I'm gonna write a letter to my poppa and my wife and tell them I found us the brains of our new outfit! (*He gives the upper bunk a friendly kick. Takes pencil and paper from under the bed.*)

ARGUE (*to us*) : The Etruscans lived and danced about a million years ago and then vanished without a trace like a high curved wave that breaks on the sand and retreats back into the sea. Poof. Vanish. Splash. (*He stabs himself and rolls away with his back to the audience.*)

NUMBER TWO (*overlapping*) : "Dear Poppa and Rita Sue . . . wait till you get this news down the old drain-pipe."

Argue's WIFE *enters writing a letter and carrying a large baby doll.*

WIFE: The baby grew another foot today and I've enrolled her in dancing class already and I've enrolled him already in prep school because it can never be too early and I tell the baby every day his Daddy is a hero and fighting all those dirty Commies in Vietnam so he can come to us and make more money for us so we can move to a bigger house and go to Yale to college and Europe on vacations and take Mommy to dances and plays and the club. Do you have any friends? Is everybody terribly tacky? Don't worry, your baby loves you and I put the heavy radio on my stomach when it plays Muzeeka and make believe it's the weight of you and then scratch the days off my calendar 'til you come home to me and the weight is really the weight of you . . . (*She exits.*)

Crowds cheer. Drums roll. EVELYN LANDIS *enters, dressed in an army jump suit and green beret. She strips off her jump suit and reveals a bikini made of streamers and newspaper columns.*

EVELYN LANDIS (*to us*): In our heart of hearts, we know God is on our side. I'm an atheist and even I got to admit God is on our side. In America God is on everybody's side! Look at Hubert Humphrey—even he gets around everything. (*She sings, and with each name, joyously rips a clump of newspaper off herself.*)
Hubert Humphrey
& Jesus Christ
Ronald Reagan
& Jesus Christ
Stokely Carmichael
& Jesus Christ
General Westmoreland
& Jesus Christ
(*The* STAGEHANDS *join in.*)
Richard Nixon
& Jesus Christ
LBJ
Was Jesus Christ
Timothy Leary
& Jesus Christ
Bonnie and Clyde
& Jesus Christ
Rocky & Romney
& Jesus Christ
Johnny Carson
& Jesus Christ
Television

& Jesus Christ
Eugene McCarthy
May be Jesus Christ

They form a line at the rear of the stage behind the double bunk. EVELYN LANDIS *and the* STAGEHANDS *keep clapping in rhythm very softly.*

NUMBER TWO (*to* ARGUE): You write that Muzeeka, huh? You're smart leaving it. It's really dull, you know? But you know when it's nice? When it's late at night and you got a bag on and you just got laid and you're driving home over the Freeway—cars above you, cars below you, lights coming at you—and you got a bag on and you turn on the car radio and the dream music starts floating in—not making any point—*not* not funny—not serious—just violins playing Begin the Beguine-y kind of music, and, late at night, your car radio starts picking up Oregon and Utah and Nevada and Canada speaking French. And Kentucky criss-crossing with Alabama. And that's all your music, huh? Dreamy. You got to stop and think where you are and you can feel the car could take right off the road and you pull back the wheel so it can lift you up and go faster and faster and dawn starts far away like a pink baby, a pink baby's backside poking up in the horizon and the air smells clean and it starts to rain and rain and the music never mounts, never builds, just stays stardustily in one mood and you love being alive. (*One of the* STAGEHANDS *uncaps a bottle of catsup and moves behind the bunk. He pours a blob of it onto the white sheet covering* NUMBER TWO. *The chorus gives a sharp "tip" sound.*) And it's raining—(*Another splotch appears on the white sheet. "Tip."*) And raining—(*More catsup; More "Tip." "Tip." "Tip." "Tip."* NUMBER TWO *sits up.*) Argue? (*The catsup catches his hand. He looks at the red of the blood.*) Argue? Argue?

Long pause.

Blackout